House Beautiful

DESIGN AND DECORATE
KITCHENS

House Beautiful

DESIGN AND DECORATE
KITCHENS

EMMA CALLERY

HEARST BOOKS
A division of Sterling Publishing Co., Inc.

New York / London
www.sterlingpublishing.com

Created, edited, and designed by
Duncan Baird Publishers Ltd.,
Castle House, 75–76 Wells Street, London W1T 3QH

Managing Editor: Emma Callery
Designer: Alison Shackleton
Illustrator: Kate Simunek

Library of Congress Cataloging-in-Publication Data

Callery, Emma.
  House beautiful design & decorate : kitchens : creating beautiful rooms from start to finish / Emma Callery.
      p. cm.
  Includes bibliographical references and index.
  ISBN-13: 978-1-58816-650-0 (alk. paper)
  ISBN-10: 1-58816-650-3 (alk. paper)
 1. Kitchens. 2. Kitchens--Designs and plans. 3. Interior decoration.
I. House beautiful. II. Title. III. Title: House beautiful design and decorate. IV. Title: Design & decorate : kitchens.
  NK2117.K5C35 2007
  747.7'97--dc22
                                        2007007271

1 2 3 4 5 6 7 8 9 10

Published by Hearst Books
A Division of Sterling Publishing Co., Inc.
387 Park Avenue South, New York, NY 10016

House Beautiful and Hearst Books are trademarks of Hearst Communications, Inc.

www.housebeautiful.com

For information about custom editions, special sales, premium and corporate purchases, please contact Sterling Special Sales Department at 800-805-5489 or specialsales@sterlingpub.com.

Distributed in Canada by Sterling Publishing
Canadian Manda Group, 165 Dufferin Street
Toronto, Ontario, Canada M6K 3H6

Distributed in Australia by Capricorn Link
(Australia) Pty. Ltd.
P.O. Box 704, Windsor, NSW 2756 Australia

Manufactured in China

Sterling ISBN 13: 978-1-58816-650-0
        ISBN 10: 1-58816-650-3

CONTENTS

Foreword

The kitchen is a key room in any house, whether it is where you quickly consume a cup of coffee before rushing to work, or the place where you relax with friends in the evening—or both. Because it has so many roles—catering center, meeting place, dining venue, a base to work and play—it can be tricky to get the look and feel right. This is where this book helps. It gives an overview of the various styles of kitchen from traditional through retro to contemporary, and the chances are you'll take elements from a few of them. And that's the point: it's all very well having a custom designed kitchen, but what you want is a kitchen designed to your needs and lifestyle. Are you a one-, two-, or even three-sink household? If the only prep you do for a meal is to tear off the packaging on a pre-cooked meal, or freshen up on the way out to a restaurant, you have different needs than someone who prepares fresh food every night, glass of wine in hand and cool music in the background.

Once you've pondered your lifestyle, there are also very practical considerations to take in, like where the drain lines are, which walls can take electrical outlets, and where all that fancy equipment is going to fit if you're not going to build an addition. Not to mention finding a color scheme that won't send you reeling straight back to bed in the morning.

The book is divided into two parts: design and decorate. The first helps you identify your style, the best layout and the infrastructure, such as lighting, electrical, floors, and the all-important issue of storage. Part two shows you how to plan the décor, choosing a color scheme and deciding how the walls will be finished together with the style of window dressing and those all-important finishing touches. Making a kitchen that is right for you is like cooking a special meal. So browse through the "ingredients" and peruse the "recipes" until you can create your own unique kitchen dish—and live with it!

Stephen Drucker, Editor in Chief, *House Beautiful*

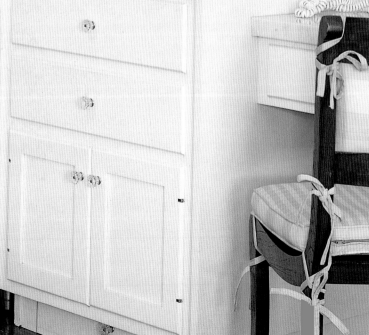

PART 1
design

be prepared

The statement "The kitchen is the heart of the home" has been made so often it has become a cliché, but, if anything, it is more true today than ever before. For many people, the kitchen is by far the most important room in the home because it is so much more than the place where food is prepared and, increasingly, consumed.

ABOVE: MANY KITCHENS ARE ENTERTAINMENT CENTERS AS WELL AS WORKING AND EATING SPACES.

OPPOSITE: GET THE STORAGE ARRANGEMENTS RIGHT AND EVERYTHING WILL HAVE ITS PLACE, SO THAT YOUR KITCHEN DOES NOT FILL UP WITH CLUTTER.

The modern kitchen is the social (some would say emotional) hub for the family, often where children play or do their homework and their parents catch up on what's happening, click out a few orders online and maybe finish some office work. However, it is often where guests congregate, making it something of a showroom, too, especially on the weekend. Property developers say that great-looking kitchens sell property. But these picture-perfect creations don't necessarily fulfil the many functions of today's kitchen. A poorly planned kitchen will be a constant source of irritation however fabulous it looks.

This section enables you to create the kitchen that is right for you, in terms of looks, use, and practicality. It starts with an overview of the different styles available. You may well decide to combine elements from two or three of them. Then the role of kitchen as working, eating, and living space is considered. The section also looks at formulating a project plan and employing kitchen designers.

The section then studies the practicalities of kitchen cabinets and equipment—the myriad choices in appliances and countertops, and all the tiny but crucial details like drawer handles. It also deals with the vital issue of storage, and gives an up-to-date briefing on your flooring and lighting options. That should provide you with all the ingredients you need to create your unique kitchen recipe: part two of this book will help you cook it into a sumptuous dish!

find your style

ABOVE: STRONG LINES AND COOL COLORS AND MATERIALS CREATE A MINIMALIST'S PARADISE.

OPPOSITE: THE WARMTH OF WOOD AND AN INTERESTING RANGE OF ITEMS ON DISPLAY MAKE FOR A COZY, WELCOMING ROOM.

Choosing a style for your kitchen can be a daunting task: the range of options is very wide and you want to be sure that you create something that will look right for at least a decade and won't be dated in a couple of years. Start by considering the period of your home, as that might guide you to a kitchen style that will suit its environment. It is often easier to determine what would be wrong: for example, a rustic-style kitchen will seem out of place in a cool, urban loft apartment. You might start by eliminating all the "wrong" looks and see what options remain.

However, it is also vital to choose a style that suits you as well as your home's architecture, and this may turn out to include elements from different periods. Of course, this happens naturally: a Shaker, Gothic, or 1950s retro kitchen will still have a microwave and a dishwasher. But by blending design elements that you like, you can create a room that is as individual as you are. The general trend is away from the uniform, fitted look to something more individual that looks as if it has evolved with the room. You could go for a quirky mix and match look, or unify the effect by painting the diverse design elements in the same or complementary colors.

As always with interior design, you also need to consider how the kitchen fits in with the rest of your home: rooms should flow into one another without shocking the senses. That doesn't mean they must look the same, but some continuity in use of materials or colors will help. A transition from a cozy living room in sophisticated shades of green to a vibrant kitchen with exotic citrus yellow walls can be rather jarring to inhabitants and guests alike.

Size and shape are factors, too: a narrow, galley-style apartment kitchen calls for clean, unfussy lines to make its limited dimensions feel bigger. In contrast, there is more scope for ornament and variety of visual interest in a larger space where you want to draw the eye around the room. Of course, the limiting factor here could be budget: it is frighteningly easy to spend vast sums on a new kitchen. However, you can achieve remarkable effects with a minor renovation by changing the décor, the style of the cabinet doors, or the furniture, and adding new touches, such as a convenient single-lever faucet.

Small details can have a major impact, too: one cost-effective trick is to buy standard cabinets but add your own more individual handles so that the look is unique to your kitchen. This melding of different elements to create a satisfying whole that reflects your own personality is the essence of good kitchen design.

Be a kitchen spy

Make your own style file by cutting out pictures of styles or features that you like from magazines and brochures. This is a good way to gather ideas and to guide yourself toward your own style preferences if you are not already aware of them. Even if the picture only shows the kind of faucet you simply must have, it will prove invaluable later on; perhaps successfully saving an agonized rushed and then regretted decision in the showroom.

BELOW: DECORATIVE THEMES ARE FUN. THIS FARMHOUSE KITCHEN FEATURES RABBITS ON THE PLATE AND THE POTTERY FIGURES ON THE WINDOWSILL.

BELOW RIGHT: MIX UP YOUR WOODS FOR A SOFTENING EFFECT. HERE DOUGLAS FIR CABINETRY COMBINES WITH AN OAK FLOOR FOR A WARM AND WELCOMING MODERN KITCHEN THAT DOESN'T LOOK STERILE.

From colonial to contemporary

This table provides a summary of how kitchen styles can blend with the main architectural styles in the United States, giving you the opportunity to match your kitchen with the age of your home.

PERIOD/STYLE OF HOME	KITCHEN STYLE	KEY MATERIALS	FEATURES	PALETTE
COLONIAL (1600–1800)	Country or Shaker	Wood (usually pine or maple)	Plain decoration	Blues and deep green, creams, gray
CLASSICAL (1740–1860)	Country	Wood	Squares and symmetrical shapes, some ornamental elements	Greens, reds, yellows, gold
VICTORIAN (1830–1880)	Traditional	Wood, tiles	Ornate flourishes, exposed hinges	Forest green, brown, mustard yellow, white
ARTS AND CRAFTS (1880–1940)	Traditional	Dark wood (often oak), colored glass	Geometric shapes, floral patterns	Violet, mint orange, brown
1950S	Retro	Ceramic tiles, painted wood, Formica	Checkerboard floor	Black, red, brown, pink, jade green
MODERN	Contemporary	Light wood, steel, glass, quartz, granite	Sleek lines, lack of embellishment, interest created by choice of materials, e.g. stainless steel	Cool, neutral, subdued tones

Small spaces call for clean, simple lines. There is more need for ornament when you want to draw the eye around a larger room.

Another source of information is your friends: you probably spend a fair bit of time in their kitchens. Which ones do you like the look of? Which feel the most spacious? What little touches make them special?

Don't be afraid to grill your friends on how they chose their own layout—people love talking about personal projects and the decisions they had to make. Make plenty of notes and take pictures for your file. In the process you will discover what you don't like (but keep it to yourself if you value your friendships!). This method of working can be invaluable when deciding on a style and especially when choosing cabinets, hardware, and appliances.

kitchen style

Most kitchen showrooms and brochures feature a basic set of styles. The most obvious element that sets the style is the cabinetry, although color and materials are important parts of the look, too, and the selection of finishing touches such as door handles can have a major impact on the end result.

ABOVE: THE CLEAN LINES OF A CONTEMPORARY KITCHEN CAN BE SOFTENED WITH FLOWERS AND OTHER SPLASHES OF COLOR.

OPPOSITE: THE KITCHEN NEEDS TO MATCH ITS SETTING. HERE THE WHITE BOARDS OF THE CEILING ARE ECHOED IN THE USE OF WHITE PANELING AND DISTRESSED WOOD.

Traditional style reflects features from the past, and is characterized by ornate, sometimes even elaborate, decorative additions combined with clean lines to create a timeless effect. Cabinet doors are deep-paneled and can be made in richly hued wood or painted cream-color to contrast with darker walls. Colors and styles can be dark and ornate, light and elegant, or a blend of the two.

The country kitchen echoes the Early American or Colonial look, which in turn evolved from traditional European design. The overall effect is best described as rustic, and should remind you of an old-style pantry. There may be a center pine table and chairs, open shelves, and a sideboard cluttered with jars of homemade pickles and jam, while the walls are hung with painted plates and pictures of farm animals. Open plate racks and large stoves are often featured.

To balance the busy effect, colors are mellow and natural: creams, greens, and browns. Countertops are made of wood. Windows have curtains rather than shades, preferably in patterned fabric. Pine, maple, birch, and other soft woods are commonly used, and floors are either wood or stone. Using some free-standing furniture, rather than having everything built-in, reinforces the country look.

Shaker

This is a highly influential utilitarian style based on furniture originally produced by the religious sect. There are Shaker elements in traditional and contemporary kitchens, but it stands as a recognizable style of its own, creating a sense of simplicity and calm. Wood—usually cherry or pine—is the main material, and doors often feature a rectangular recessed panel surrounded by a wide flat frame to form an unfussy, plain adornment. Wooden pegs mounted on a flat board are another classic Shaker element. Colors include soft tones of yellow, blue, and gray.

Retro

Retro is a high-impact look that harkens back to the polished chrome diners of the 1950s. Built-in kitchens were the trend at that time, so the look is dominated by matching wall-to-wall cabinets. The formal effect is softened by the choice of colors: contrasting blacks and reds, a choice of pinks and browns with pistachio and jade greens, and blues. Bright plastic laminate countertops set the stage for a variety of small chrome appliances, such as a toaster, tea kettle, and coffeemaker. Edges are stylishly rounded. The classic retro floor is a black or red and white checkerboard pattern in linoleum or vinyl.

Contemporary

The classic contemporary look is sleek and minimal, with most of the kitchen apparatus hidden away or exploited as a feature in its own right, such as a café-style coffee machine. Indeed, much of the equipment in a contemporary kitchen looks as if it has been borrowed from the chef of the nearest restaurant. Appliances are finished in stainless steel or other metals; countertops should be granite or marble with steel, aluminum, or ceramic mosaic backsplashes; and there should be plenty of frosted glass used for shelves or cabinet faces. The effect is softened by the pale wood of the cabinets (often plainly decorated in the Shaker style) and the wood or tile floor. Slatted shades fit snugly into the window recesses.

While many contemporary kitchens are made up of built-in units (often without toe-kicks), there is a trend toward choosing a mixture of freestanding units for a more individual effect. Clutter is out, and consequently there must be abundant storage so that all but a few key items are hidden away—leaving a selection of utensils hanging over the range or displayed on metal racks for the quintessential industrial look. Joints are flush for a seamless finish. The danger with going for the high-tech chic of a contemporary look is that it can look dated within a few years—and most kitchens should last 10–15 years before a major overhaul is required.

CONTEMPORARY KITCHENS HAVE THE COOL, ORGANIZED FEEL OF A PROFESSIONAL KITCHEN. THE MATCHING UNDERSTATED DETAILS ON THE CABINET DOORS AND DRAWERS AND TINIEST OF HANDLES HAVE AN AIR OF EFFICIENCY, WHILE THE PLAIN, UNADORNED SHELF RUNNING THE LENGTH OF THE KITCHEN ENSURES THAT DISHES AND GLASSES CAN BE USED AT A MOMENT'S NOTICE.

kitchen roles

Kitchens have different roles according to the time of day, the day of the week, and the stage of life of those who live in the house. Each role makes different requirements of the room. For example, a young family will probably gather in the morning for a large breakfast—which means the room should have a suitable seating area—when a few years down the line, with the kids having left home, there may be two "empty nesters" cozily waking up over coffee and pastries.

Few things are more frustrating than the realization that your dream kitchen no longer meets your changing needs. It may help to write down or at least consider the answers to these questions: Who will use the kitchen? What will each of them use it for? What will they need in the room? How often will they need it? Is this likely to change?

ABOVE: SETTING ASIDE AN AREA FOR INFORMAL FAMILY DINING MAKES IT EASY FOR THE COOK TO CHAT WITH OTHERS WHILE PREPARING THE MEAL, AND SERVING IT IS A CINCH!

OPPOSITE: BAR STOOLS AT THE COUNTER ALLOW FOR EASY SNACKING AND INFORMAL BREAKFASTS. AT THE SAME TIME, THE ANGLED COUNTERTOP HELPS DELINEATE THE AREA AND PROVIDES MORE SPACE FOR THE REST OF THE ROOM.

The primary function of the kitchen is as the place where food is stored and prepared. However elegant the room looks, if you can't cook a meal in it easily, it isn't right. The usual starting point when designing from a workplace perspective is to consider the "work triangle" of sink (with the dishwasher close by), cooktop (or stove), and refrigerator—the three points you move between most when cooking. Your aim is to minimize the number of steps you need to take between these three points to save you energy and time and to reduce the amount of lifting and carrying required, so they should form a triangle rather than a straight line. If you have a separate cooktop and wall oven and one of these work stations must be further away, make it the oven as that is used less.

The aim is to minimize traffic flow between the zones so that the cook's shoes don't wear out too quickly!

Zone sweet zone

Another way of considering the design is to think in terms of zones:

• **The hot area where you cook** The key part of the room where the chef will spend much of his or her time.

• **The wet area for washing** Dishwashers can't cope with every item of kitchen equipment (for example, they are rarely large enough for baking trays, and will blunt sharp knives), so the sink remains important for cleaning equipment as well as rinsing vegetables.

• **The prep area where you get the food ready** This needs to be as spacious as possible, clean, and free of clutter.

• **The storage areas for equipment and food, both refrigerated and pantry** Crucial for stress-free cooking, the positioning will vary according to need, but the choices made also have a major aesthetic impact.

Save your feet

Clearly, the aim is to minimize traffic flow between these zones so that the cook doesn't wear out his or her shoes every time a meal is being prepared. Furthermore, the less distance the cook travels, the less mess is made, because of the reduced scope for dropping or spilling things. Similarly, the more countertop area you have, the more room there is to make a mess, and the more surface will need to be wiped down. So, a well-planned kitchen with short distances between zones, or a "tight triangle," is easier to use and to keep clean.

Professional chefs opt for a galley in which they simply turn to face the stove or the sink and are within an arm's length of a countertop for prepping. This isn't possible (or aesthetically desirable) in most kitchens, and anyway you probably haven't got an army of sous chefs and dishwashers to support you, but the important idea is to plan for minimal footwork when cooking.

 THIS ISLAND COMBINES A PRACTICAL WORKING AREA WITH A PLACE TO EAT OR READ.

 STORING PANS NEAR WHERE THEY WILL BE USED SAVES A LOT OF SHOE LEATHER.

 MAKE THE MOST OF NATURAL LIGHT BY SITING THE SINK UNDER THE WINDOW.

4 IT'S A SHORT TRIP FROM COOKTOP AND TOASTER TO ISLAND SNACKING STATION.

ABOVE: DEFINE AN IN-KITCHEN
DINING AREA WITH ITS OWN
LIGHTING AND COLOR, AS HERE
WITH THE ORNATE CHANDELIER
ABOVE AN EXOTIC LIME-COLORED
TABLE THAT CONTRASTS SO
SPECTACULARLY WITH THE PINK
FURNISHINGS AND SPLASHBACK.

OPPOSITE: A PAIR OF SINKS
ALLOWS YOU TO USE ONE FOR
PREPARING FOOD AND THE OTHER
FOR WASHING POTS. IT IS ALSO
IDEAL FOR WHEN THERE ARE TWO
COOKS ON THE GO.

Two's company

Another factor is that many homes are inhabited by couples who share the cooking, sometimes at the same time—so one will prepare an entrée while the other completes the dessert. They'll need space for their individual tasks and won't want to keep bumping into each other, so the design will require two countertops separated by one point of the work triangle. One of the prep areas could be an island, possibly a moveable one (see page 35 for more on islands).

Such lifestyle issues can have other ramifications for the design: maybe you need two separate sinks, a pair of refrigerators so that your paths do not keep crossing, or two ovens. Furthermore, two people might need to do two different jobs at the same time: one might be unloading the dishwasher while the other is rolling out pastry. Think through the way you like to work in your kitchen and if there are two avid cooks, aim to reduce the interference between them.

Kitchens to eat in

Naturally, we like to eat in the kitchen, whether it is a quick breakfast, a mid-morning snack, a light lunch with friends, mid-afternoon tea, or the evening meal. Depending on the lifestyle of the household, a breakfast bar or island might suffice. However, even in houses with a dining room, people sometimes prefer the ease and informality of kitchen dining, especially during the week, and indeed there is a marked trend away from dining rooms in American homes.

This calls for a large kitchen capable of providing sufficient space for people to sit comfortably around one big table.

Sometimes the socializing is more formal, with guests coming into the kitchen for drinks, snacks, and company, which is far nicer for the cook, who can then chat with the visitors rather than be shut away in another room. However, the guests need space to circulate, and somewhere to sit or at least to put their drinks. The host will want the room to look attractive and neat, creating a need for plenty of storage and a pleasing overall look to the room. If guests also dine in the kitchen, a large table is required and the décor, or at least the lighting options, will need to be suitable for this type of entertaining.

Kitchens as living spaces

Today's kitchens are more than food preparation areas, however important that is. The people in the house tend to gravitate toward the kitchen because it is usually warm and a source of drinks, snacks, and company. So the kitchen becomes a socializing space where news is exchanged, messages delivered, and family members interact every day. This has design implications: family members and friends will want to sit somewhere, probably at a table, and be able to face everybody else. An example of how different this is from the recent past is the fact that sinks were once positioned under a window so that mothers could enjoy the view into the yard and keep an eye on the children playing. Now sinks often face into the central space so that whoever is washing up can see and communicate with the other people in the room, and maintain a sentry's view of the children in the room.

The kitchen often becomes a work space for non-cooking activities, too—children's homework, sewing, painting are all possibilities—and a computer is now a part of many kitchens, used for work, play, surfing the net, and even running the household budget. This is in addition to the almost standard practice of having a television in the kitchen—or at least a radio. Cooks who are sports fans have been known to install large-screen TVs hidden behind kitchen cabinet doors so that they can put together a meal without missing the big game.

One way of making the kitchen truly inviting is to have a comfortable sofa in addition to the usual kitchen chairs—assuming you have the space, of course.

WITH ITS BREAKFAST BAR AND DINING TABLE BEYOND, THIS KITCHEN IS CLEVERLY DESIGNED TO GIVE PLENTY OF SEATING OPTIONS. NOTICE HOW THE STONE FLOOR AND MOSAICS OF THE WORKING END ARE SOFTENED BY WALLPAPER AND CURTAINS WHERE FAMILY AND FRIENDS SIT AND RELAX.

ABOVE: IN A LARGE ROOM, THE
KITCHEN AREA CAN CO-EXIST
HAPPILY WITH OTHER LIVING
SPACES. USE DIFFERENT FLOOR
MATERIALS AND LIGHTS TO MARK
EACH AREA'S PURPOSE.

This also offers a relaxing spot for the non-cook (and, indeed, for the busy chef when that break is earned), and really helps to transform even the busiest kitchen into a living space that all can share and enjoy.

Many homes have an open-plan arrangement where the living room and kitchen are not separated by walls but divided by the décor scheme. The many advantages this offers in terms of lifestyle flexibility are countered by the problem that cooking odors tend to invade the living space. The answer is good ventilation and an excellent exhaust hood—which, again, must be built into the design.

Kitchens and kids

If there are children in the household, their needs will influence the kitchen plan. Snacks will need to be consumed out of the way of a busy cook. The kitchen table may become the homework desk, while the walls or other surfaces are adorned with artwork. A lower level working surface makes it easier for small hands to get cooking (there is more on multilevel surfaces on pages 40 and 75).

It also often makes sense to have access to the yard direct from the kitchen so that you can still supervise young play, but, if possible, also to have entry via an adjacent mudroom where boots and raincoats can be stored.

ABOVE: A MINI-WORK STATION IS A MAJOR ASSET IN KITCHENS WHERE WORK AND LEISURE MEET. SET AT ONE END OF THE ROOM, IT IS EASY TO ACCESS, YET DOES NOT DISTRACT FROM THE MAIN PURPOSE OF THE KITCHEN—FOOD PREPARATION.

RIGHT: HAVING A PET MIGHT AFFECT YOUR DESIGN. FOR EXAMPLE, YOU MIGHT CONSIDER HAVING A SEPARATE FEEDING AREA. SOME KITCHENS HAVE BUILT-IN FEEDERS SET INTO DRAWERS FOR EASY ACCESS THAT CAN BE HIDDEN AWAY WHEN NOT NEEDED.

Kids in the kitchen

A number of design points help make the kitchen safer for kids:
- **Use a high chair** with a safety harness.
- **Have childproof safety covers** for electrical outlets.
- **Store glass and sharp objects** out of reach, or in lockable drawers and cabinets—even aluminum foil or plastic wrap dispensers have sharp teeth.
- **Keep cleaning solvents and sprays** out of reach.
- **Install lock-out options on appliances** so that little hands can't switch them on.
- **Install automatic shut-off devices,** which have a timer to switch off any appliances that have been left on. Have lock-out switches on ranges, ovens, and dishwashers.
- **Put anti-scald devices on faucets.**
- **Choose round or curved countertop edges and corners,** especially on islands and peninsulas, to ensure there are no sharp edges at child's head height.
- **Don't have an overhanging tablecloth** that the child could pull on.
- **Put trash cans inside a cabinet with a locking door**—there could be sharp-edged metal lids and other dangers in there.
- **Have a safe storage place for plastic bags,** as they are a choking hazard.
- **Plan to include a multi-level counter** with a lower surface for children to work at, or buy a step stool for them to come up to a comfortable height.

If there are children in the household, their needs must be part of the overall kitchen plan.

ARRANGING SEATING NEAR THE COOKING STATION ALLOWS THE COOK TO BE FRIENDLY AND STILL GET THE WORK DONE. THE SLIGHTLY LOWER TABLE ADJACENT TO THE ISLAND FREES THE COUNTERTOP FOR PREPARATION AND DISPLAY.

plan the layout

ABOVE: WITH A UNIT LIKE THIS, THE COOK CAN WASH, PREPARE, AND HEAT FOOD WITHOUT MOVING HIS OR HER FEET.

OPPOSITE: THIS LARGE TABLE PROVIDES AN EXCELLENT WORKING SURFACE, BATHED IN NATURAL LIGHT FROM THE LARGE WINDOW. YOU CAN NEVER HAVE ENOUGH WORK SURFACES, SO PLAN TO INCLUDE AS MUCH AS YOU CAN.

The layout of your kitchen is far more important than the décor, because once it is set you can rarely make major changes to the placement of things, while you can transform the look of a kitchen with a couple of cans of paint. In this section, we consider kitchen shapes, prioritizing what you really need and what you would like to have, and addressing some practicalities about kitchen design. Then it's a question of research and deciding whether you need professional help from a kitchen designer.

If your kitchen suffers from lack of light or space, you may want to consider making changes in the walls. These could include: removing walls altogether to unite the kitchen and dining area; creating half walls that divide space but leave it open and airy; adding windows—even a small one to the outside or to a mudroom can allow more precious natural light in; rebuilding a wall using glass bricks, which allow light through but not clear images, and can add a fresh sense of space and light in a modern setting.

Structural change won't be cheap, but it could be cost-effective. Remember that some walls are supporting or structural, which help hold up the house, so you can't remove them. These usually run perpendicular to the roof rafters or trusses. Depending on how much work you are planning, you should consult an architect or structural engineer, as removing a supporting wall could result in structural repercussions elsewhere in your home.

Non-load-bearing walls, which often separate rooms, are called partition walls. They usually run parallel to the rafter or trusses and can be changed or removed safely. Remember that many electrical wires are routed inside walls and that the rerouting will involve cutting out a channel in the plaster or making holes in the wallboard, which will then need to be repaired: definitely a job for a professional.

In a large kitchen you could also consider installing sliding walls, which create an open-plan room when pulled back, but can be closed to make the space on each side more private.

Windows A major remodelling project includes the opportunity to enlarge, add, or reconfigure the windows and it is certainly worth considering this. You may want to have a brighter, sunnier room at breakfast time, or be able to sip a glass of wine while enjoying the sunset, or be able to get rid of heat, smoke, or odors by throwing open a couple of windows to create a draft.

It usually makes sense to stick mainly to the types of window already installed in your home and neighborhood, otherwise your property can look a little out of place. There are several types of standard window (see opposite); exceptions are known as specialty windows.

You may want to replace the glass with a more modern energy-efficient, better insulated arrangement: new windows can be dual- or even triple-glazed, with the gap between panes filled with argon gas, and the glass low-E (low-emission) coated to lessen the passage of heat. These windows also cushion sound, so they are desirable if you live near a busy road or railroad track.

Even if you decide your windows are just fine where they are, they'll need varnishing or painting (unless they're aluminum or solid vinyl) and new window treatments to fit in with your new décor.

1 THE FURNITURE AND WINDOW TRIM ARE PAINTED IN MATCHING MEDITERRANEAN BLUE, MAKING THE MOST OF THE SMALL WINDOW.

2 MAXIMIZE THE FLOW OF LIGHT THROUGH SMALL SPACES BY USING REFLECTIVE MATERIALS, SUCH AS STAINLESS STEEL AND LIGHT COLORS.

3 WINDOW MUNTINS IMBUE A SENSE OF HISTORY AND BRING A PERIOD FEEL TO THIS MUCH-MODERNIZED CONTEMPORARY ROOM.

Window options

Small details can cause major irritation, so if you are fitting new windows, choose carefully from these options.

Awning Hinged at the top to open horizontally, this style is very good for providing that kitchen essential, ventilation, above picture windows. It suits any kitchen style.

Casement This is an outward-opening, hinged window, mostly identified with twentieth-century homes and not suitable for period properties. Larger windows can be opened and shut by a hand-crank mechanism.

Double or single hung This features a pair or one moveable sash, which slides vertically within the frame. It fits in with all kitchen styles apart from the most contemporary look.

A picture window doesn't open. It can be one pane of glass, or be divided by muntins. It suits most styles, but for a contemporary look, don't use muntins.

Skylight A window in the roof, providing light and offering a view of the sky. It is only possible in single-story kitchen additions or top-floor apartments and is best positioned near the edge of a room so the light reflects off walls.

Sliding A window that slides horizontally. This can be a valuable space saver and works best with modern styles.

Specialty This is a window shaped—round, half round, or triangular—to echo other shapes in the room and contribute to the overall effect. Such an unusual shape can be used as a striking feature as well as having the practical benefit of allowing light into the kitchen.

THE OWNERS WISELY KEPT THE LARGE WINDOW AND DECIDED AGAINST ADDING A SHADE OR CURTAIN TO ALLOW AS MUCH LIGHT AS POSSIBLE TO FLOOD INTO THIS COMPACT ROOM.

Few modern kitchens are without an island, a feature that fulfills many roles.

What shape should your kitchen be?

The shape will be dictated in part by the dimensions and proportions of the space available, with the other factor being your kitchen lifestyle.

Kitchen shape	Description	Advantages	Layout options	Socializing options
Single file or counter	Kitchen along one wall	Very cost effective; good for single-person households	None: equipment is in line, so cannot create a work triangle	Poor: cook faces the wall all the time and no room for guests
Double file (galley or corridor)	Two rows of cabinets along opposite walls	Usually economical to build	Stove and sink on one side, refrigerator on the other	Poor, unless a folding table can be installed at one end; corridor can be a busy pathway
L-shape	Two walls at right angles	More spacious; offers room for non-cooks; easier to arrange	Easy to form a work triangle (but this can become stretched); island adds options	Good if space allows room for a table
U-shape	Three walls forming an open square	Continuous counter space with plenty of storage options	One work station on each wall, with the sink in the middle and the refrigerator right on the end; island adds options	Good if space allows, but need to position the table away from the work triangle so it doesn't block access
G-shape	U-shaped with a peninsula forming a short "fourth wall"	Block shape offers many options; extra space is a good format for two-cook kitchens	Very flexible, allowing for choice of work stations	Cook can be cut off from others in room depending on the layout

Galley kitchens

The narrow dimensions of a galley kitchen dictate the positioning of appliances, making it fairly easy to determine where they will go. The emphasis is on accentuating what space there is by creating clean lines and providing as much storage as possible behind plain doors (busy patterns make the room seem smaller, so the floor should also be fairly plain). Fold away chopping boards, stools rather than chairs, and collapsible tables will help prevent a sense of claustrophobia. Pocket or folding doors save space—or perhaps you can dispense with the door altogether.

Islands

Kitchen islands are a major trend in kitchen design, and it seems that few modern kitchens are complete without one. This is a large, permanent addition, always with a worktop, but often also housing a cooktop, a sink, or a small refrigerator—perhaps one just for beverages for thirsty people to raid without bumping into the chef. Remember that the island may require plumbing, ventilation, and an electricity supply if it is fitted with appliances or a sink.

Islands can tighten up the work triangle in a large kitchen while also serving as a visual and social focal point. A major benefit is the additional storage offered, either with base cabinets, drawers, or open shelving (which also provides an opportunity for display). Another plus is that the island can incorporate an eating space, perfect for

1 AN ISLAND IS A GREAT PLACE TO STOP OFF FOR A QUICK SNACK THAT HAS BEEN PREPARED WITHIN WHISPERING DISTANCE A FEW FEET AWAY.

2 AN ISLAND IS PARADISE WHEN STORAGE ELSEWHERE IS IN SHORT SUPPLY. THIS COMPACT UNIT HAS BEEN USED TO DISPLAY FAVORITE PIECES AS WELL AS FOR STORAGE.

3 UNUSUAL ISLANDS ADD CHARACTER. THIS IMPOSING COLONIAL-STYLE TABLE WITH A CONTEMPORARY STAINLESS STEEL ADDITION WAS IMPORTED TO THIS KITCHEN FROM AFRICA.

informal dining, snacking, or gathering for a talk and a drink. The island can add to the sociable nature of a kitchen by allowing the cook to work at it while facing into the room where the children or guests congregate. Furthermore, an island allows you to enlarge the work or dining area, and helps to link the food preparation and eating areas, making the kitchen seem more unified.

Grander kitchens sometimes have two islands: a main one with a cooktop and eating area, with a smaller one housing a sink and a beverage refrigerator. At the other end of the scale, if there isn't enough space for an island but you like its advantages, try a rolling cart or a mobile butcher's block, which can be wheeled away when not in use (though you'll have to think about where it will go—perhaps it can double up as a peninsula end).

Locating a permanent island correctly is crucial: an island that interrupts free movement becomes a block, especially if it has no obvious function.

Planning for cleanliness

The kitchen presents the toughest cleaning job in the home. Installing a new kitchen offers many opportunities to make cleaning routines easier. Less traffic means fewer spills, so a well-planned work triangle with strategically placed countertop space will limit the amount of cleaning required, but there are other tricks to consider.

Good ventilation reduces moisture and means that any dirt will be dry, which is much easier to remove. Seams and joints are dirt magnets, so keep them to a minimum and build in curves on the joints between floor and toe-kick and between countertops and walls so that there is no right angle where it can collect. Similarly, there are less dirt traps in a kitchen with built-in appliances compared to one with freestanding units as these have gaps around them.

Make sure the countertop overhangs cabinet doors and drawers so that liquids do not drip down into them. Sinks undermounted below countertops are far more convenient as dirt can simply be swept into them.

Go for flat decoration on doors rather than raised paneling or elaborate moldings, both of which will gather dirt. Pulls and handles make it less likely that grease will accumulate on cabinet doors, which is otherwise hard to avoid as they will be touched so frequently. Drawers that open out fully are much easier to keep clean and tidy, and cabinets attract less interior dirt than open shelves.

A large chopping board is very user-friendly as cuttings can be swept off easily, preferably into an integrated trash collector, making cleaning up a smooth operation.

OPPOSITE: AN ISLAND UNIT ON WHEELS IS MORE VERSATILE THAN A CONVENTIONAL FIXED ISLAND BECAUSE IT CAN BE MOVED AROUND THE ROOM. THE WHEELS ALSO MAKE IT MUCH EASIER TO CLEAN THE FLOOR UNDERNEATH IT.

Right location, wrong space

If the space available isn't right for what you want, you'll either have to compromise or consider changes to the building. Maybe you can knock down a wall into the adjacent mudroom or butler's pantry to increase the amount of space or light available? Or remove part of it to create a half wall? Can you afford to build an addition? If not, don't despair: the smallest kitchens can look great and function well. It's all down to the planning. Consult your style file (see pages 14–15) and visit showrooms specifically looking for ideas rather than for what to buy. This can give you a different perspective when viewing, as sometimes styles and colors that don't appeal to you can put you off an excellent design that meets your needs. Finally, remember that symmetry is always pleasing to the eye, and having a focal point (such as the range) with shapes and contours balanced on either side of it, is likely to create a "feel good" kitchen.

Another important thing you must consider before furthering the plan is the amount and sources of natural light in the kitchen. Direct sunlight is particularly welcome over the breakfast table, guaranteed to bring cheer to even the sleepiest start to the day, and ideally kitchens should have plenty of access to the outdoors, for views, light, and ventilation. This is likely to influence the whole layout—the overall shape, placement of appliances, and the location of cabinets. Information on lighting is included on pages 100–107.

NATURAL LIGHT BRINGS A ROOM TO LIFE. WHAT COULD BE A STERN AND UNWELCOMING BLACK AND WHITE COLOR SCHEME BATHES IN THE WARM GLOW OF SUNLIGHT STREAMING THROUGH THE MANY WINDOWS. BY NIGHT, ITS MANY CEILING LIGHTS ENSURE THE KITCHEN REMAINS BRIGHT AND CHEERFUL.

Unless you are building an addition to house the kitchen, there will already be internal pipes, drainpipes, electrical switches, and venting ductwork in place. These can usually be relocated, but this will add to the cost. As a general rule, appliances that require plumbing should all be positioned along the same wall. If you can adapt to at least some of the existing infrastructure, you might have more in your budget for the finishing touches.

While thinking about practicalities, and especially if you are already living in the kitchen space, place boxes and chairs to represent an island, a peninsula, or other planned features that you will have to navigate. You might realize they are more trouble than they are worth because they block a necessary pathway.

Up to the task

At this stage it is also worth considering whether some surfaces should be at different levels. For example, a tall pastry cook will work more comfortably on a slightly higher countertop, while a cook who prefers to sit while chopping and slicing may require a lower work surface—and any children likely to be cooking in the room will also be more comfortable at this level. There is an aesthetic advantage, too, for multiiple levels add a new dimension to the look of the kitchen, enhancing the sense of depth and creating visual interest.

Must have, want, or got it already?

Now you can prepare two lists: things you must have, and the things you'd like to have if possible. This is useful in guiding the design forward. Is the plasma TV essential and should it be hidden in a cabinet, or could you live without it? Would your kitchen still work well without a steam oven? The must-haves should include all aspects of the design: if the panoramic view is the reason you bought the house, you'll want to enjoy it over breakfast. The aim is to include all the "must haves" and as many "wants" as possible in the end result.

Consider also what you already have in the kitchen. If the appliances are in good condition, the flooring does a fine job, or the countertop is bearing up well, you don't necessarily need to change them so long as they fit in with the new design. Would repair and renovation be sufficient for some items?

Decide what you must have, and what you want: the first is your priority, the second a luxury.

1 A RANGE OF LEVELS MAKES THE ROOM MORE INTERESTING AS THE EYE IS DRAWN AROUND THE SPACE.

2 BALANCE IS PLEASING TO THE EYE, AND THE BLENDING OF SHAPES AND MATERIALS CREATES A HARMONIZING WHOLE.

3 THIS DESIGN MAKES THE MOST OF EVERY CORNER AND UTILIZES ALL THE HEIGHT OF A RELATIVELY SMALL SPACE.

4 OPEN SHELVES DON'T SUIT ALL PEOPLE: FOR FLEXIBILITY, INSTALL CABINETS WITH DOORS, TOO.

On to the drawing board

Now you are ready to rough out your design. At the very least, sketch it out, even if you can't do it to scale. If you have the skills, create a template of the kitchen space on graph paper and cut out the countertop and appliance shapes to scale from heavy paper: this allows you to adjust positions as your design evolves (which you can be sure it will!).

Alternatively, take accurate measurements (the saying in the trade is, "measure twice, cut once") and your rough sketch to a home center that offers a design service. Don't be afraid to do this more than once: it is part of the deal for them and they know that if they get it right, you're likely to become a valuable customer.

Once the home center has drawn up your design and you've selected your appliances and cabinetry, they'll be able to cost the job. This commonly leads to a revision of your plan: you may need to scale down your desires, or you might find you can afford more from your "wants" list. Much depends on the choices you make of materials, finishes, and appliances.

If the price comes in higher than you expected and you need to make cuts rather than raise extra finance, consider the following:

• **New cabinets** often take up about half the total budget. Is there a cheaper option or could you even paint or refurbish the existing ones (see page 76)?
• **A smart granite countertop** can be replaced by a cheaper lookalike.
• **Laminate or resilient flooring** can match the look of more expensive wood or stone.

The safe kitchen

The combination of sharp knives, heavy items, heat, water, and electrical appliances makes the kitchen the most dangerous place in the house. Here are some tips to make it more safe. See also the advice on kids in the kitchen (page 29).

- *Place a fire extinguisher near a door exit.*

- *Install smoke alarms near the kitchen.*

- *Light working areas properly, avoiding glare or shadow.*

- *Use non-slip flooring, such as matte-finished wood, textured vinyl, or textured ceramic tiles.*

- *Use non-skid backing on rugs.*

- *Position microwaves so that you can remove hot food without having to stretch.*

- *Have the sink close to the cooktop for easy draining of pans.*

- *Check that the cooktop you are planning to buy has a surface indicator.*

- *Have at least 18 inches of countertop on either side of a cooktop so that handles can be turned away from the heat.*

- *Identify where hot dishes, pots, and trays will be placed when removed from the oven or microwave.*

- *Avoid flammable material on windows close to hot appliances.*

- *Store heavy items, such as pans, at waist to knee level.*

- *Consider installing the dishwasher a foot or so above floor level so that you don't have to bend to fill and empty it, and so that the open door is more visible.*

- *Always place knives blade down in dishwasher racks.*

- *Have soft-action, under-mounted drawer glides so that fingers can't be trapped.*

- *Use a small folding step stool for reaching the contents of high cabinets.*

- *Ensure wheel mechanisms of rolling carts are easy to lock.*

BE PREPARED TO EXPERIMENT WITH LAYOUTS. FOR EXAMPLE, THIS TABLE COULD BE POSITIONED IN SEVERAL WAYS. MARK OUT SHAPES AND WALK AROUND THEM TO GET A FEEL FOR HOW THEY WOULD WORK.

OPPOSITE: ASK A DESIGNER TO ADVISE YOU ON HOW TO USE COLOR TO BEST EFFECT. THIS MAINLY WHITE KITCHEN HAS HAD COLOR INTRODUCED THROUGH THE GREEN TILED BACKSPLASH AND CREAM STONE FLOOR. ICE-CREAM-COLORED LACQUERED STOOLS ADD BRIGHTER (AND MOVEABLE) TONES TO THE ROOM.

• **Replacing appliances** can be a luxury. You could always postpone such purchases for a while and use the old ones, provided you're not relocating them.
• **Labor costs** are a big part of most budgets. Perhaps you can handle the demolition and painting.

Do I need a kitchen designer?

Kitchen manufacturers are willing to offer plenty of advice, but inevitably it will be geared to selling you some of their products. There are a number of reasons it may be worth employing a kitchen designer yourself:
• **You are more likely to get the kitchen you want,** rather than the one someone else wants to sell you.
• **Experience enables a designer to make suggestions** that you might not have thought of.
• **A designer knows what things should cost,** and may be able to negotiate better deals than you can.
• **A designer will know the current legal minimum standards** with which you must comply.

You have a choice on paying for the designer's time for input on ideas, or asking him or her to oversee the whole project, acting as your link with any contractors. On a big job, a specialist designer can save you a lot of time and heartache, but of course there is a fee for this, which will come out of your kitchen budget.

Personal recommendation is the best way to find a good kitchen designer, so don't hesitate to ask friends and contacts. They may also be able to inform you how flexible the arrangement was and how well the designer stuck to the estimate. You can also contact the National Kitchen and Bath Association via their website: www.nkba.org. This trade association runs a certification program for kitchen designers so you know they'll be up to the job. However, bear in mind that not every good designer chooses to obtain this stringent qualification.

Decide how much help you need. Maybe you want advice on choosing fixtures and appliances, or maybe the focus is on décor. Make your needs clear, and when sounding out a designer, find out:
• **How much experience** he or she has in domestic kitchen design.
• **Does he or she design kitchens** in the style you are planning
• **What will the payment arrangements be?**
• **Is work subcontracted** or done by the designer's own employees?
Choose someone you are comfortable having in your home: kitchen design requires a working relationship that calls for trust and good communication, and if you have doubts over these elements, go for someone else.

kitchen contents

ABOVE: SMALL DETAILS COUNT,
LIKE THE WAY THE DOOR
HARDWARE ECHOES THE
STAINLESS STEEL OF THE STOVE.

OPPOSITE: THE CONTENTS OF
THIS BOOKSHELF ACTIVELY
CONTRIBUTE TO THE DÉCOR.

One of the difficulties of kitchen renovation is that you are faced with decision after decision on exactly what you want and where, and it is easy to lose focus and make hurried, poor choices that you'll later regret. This section takes you through all the contents of your kitchen: the countertops, sinks, appliances, and cabinets, together with other storage and their hardware.

Even small details can have a major impact on the end result, and the choice of cabinet finish is crucial (and usually a major part of the budget) to the end result. Follow the advice on researching and choosing a style just as carefully for all these elements of your kitchen.

The vast majority of kitchen renovations include a change of countertop. This is partly because the countertop suffers the brunt of wear and tear: a combined attack of heat, steam, impact, oil, stains, and abrasive cleaners is bound to take its toll. However, in addition to being able to survive all this, the countertop is a highly visible surface and it needs to look good and complement the rest of the room. The table overleaf summarizes some key points about each material: its main features and its heat, stain, and scratch resistance.

Countertops are the stars of the kitchen: able to handle a demanding role and still come up shining.

Countertop lowdown

Looks aren't everything. Countertops have to cope with knives, water, oil, food colors, the hurly-burly of kitchen life, and still look great. Here's the lowdown on the most popular material choices.

Material	Features	Heat resistance	Stain resistance	Scratch resistance
Ceramic tile	Wide range of finishes; easy to maintain	Good	Good, but grouting can discolor	Can chip or crack
Concrete	Can be any color	Fair	Fair	Poor
Granite	Stylish and very durable; requires regular resealing	Good	Good	Fair
Laminate	Wide range of colors; easy to clean	Can be poor	Reasonable	Poor
Marble	Looks great; stays cool —perfect for rolling out pastry; requires regular resealing	Good	Poor	Poor
Quartz	Wide range of colors and finishes; easy to maintain, but you must use special cleaning products	Poor	Good	Good
Solid surfacing	Many colors plus can mimic the look of stone	Reasonable	Good	Good
Steel	Matches stainless steel appliances and fittings; easy to maintain	Good	Good	Poor
Wood	Stylish; good surface for chopping and slicing; must be oiled regularly	Poor	Poor	Poor

Countertops and backsplashes

All of the following materials, apart from concrete, can also be used for the backsplash, and another option is glass tiles. The choice is whether to go for contrast (such as ceramic tiles behind a laminate countertop) to add interest or use the same material for both, for a sleek, streamlined effect. The contrast of colors and/or textures is generally more appealing, and the backsplash offers a chance to give the décor a lift with a striking accent color (see page 114). You can mix materials by having, say, a metal backsplash behind the sink and granite above the countertop.

Ceramic tile These pieces of fired clay can be glazed to create many colors and textures and are relatively cheap. They are especially popular when a patterned look is desired. However, the grout lines can be discolored by dirt and tiles can chip. The uneven surface makes chopping and slicing tricky.

Concrete This is a thick, seamless layer of concrete offering the benefit of being customized to any color and texture you like. As durable as stone, it is becoming popular in contemporary kitchens. It requires sealing to cope with stains and heat.

Granite This is the most popular stone used for countertops. It looks stylish and is very durable. It must be resealed regularly, and glossy finishes can show water spots.

BELOW LEFT: CERAMIC TILE COUNTERTOPS HAVE THE BENEFIT OF MATCHING SIMILAR MATERIALS ON WALLS AND BACKSPLASHES, BRINGING A SENSE OF UNITY TO THE KITCHEN.

BELOW: THE REFLECTIVE QUALITY OF STAINLESS STEEL HAS LIGHT-ENHANCING PROPERTIES. IT ALSO GIVES THE KITCHEN A SLEEK, CONTEMPORARY FINISH.

ABOVE: CERAMIC TILES MAKE GREAT BACKSPLASHES (BUT WATCH OUT FOR GROUT STAINS).

OPPOSITE: MARBLE WORKS WITH ANYTHING. HERE THE ISLAND COUNTERTOP HARMONIZES WITH THE DARK WOOD AND THE DISTINCTIVE CHECKERBOARD-STYLE BACKSPLASH.

Laminates Plastic laminate is a popular material for countertops because it is cheap, cheap, and comes in a wide range of colors, textures, and patterns. It is comprised of a thick polymer layer bonded to plywood or particleboard. The lower the price, the thinner the plastic layer, meaning scratches show more readily and it has less heat resistance. Over time, water can infiltrate joins, causing discoloring and peeling.

Marble and other stone Marble is an elegant, smooth stone that is great for rolling out pastry because it stays so cool. However, it is unforgiving of stains and scratches and is very expensive. Other natural stones, such as soapstone, slate, and limestone, are also popular. They come in a variety of colors but like all stone are porous, so must be sealed, and tend to scratch easily.

Quartz This is made by grinding up quartz crystals and heat-bonding them with acrylic or resin and colorants. Quartz is a highly durable material offering many colors and finishes at a lower price than stone. Its drawback: poor heat resistance.

Solid surfacing These are blocks of polyester or acrylic resins (or a blend of the two), so they have no substrate like a laminate and are more scratch-resistant and likely to last longer. This is reflected in the price. Many finishes are available but solid surfacing is particularly good at replicating the look of natural stone.

Stainless steel This metal coordinates well and is ideal for industrial-style contemporary kitchens, but scratches and fingerprints show up and diminish its sleek appeal. It is also quite noisy to work on.

Wood Butcher's block made from hard wood, such as maple, oak, or beech, has a warm, stylish look and is the perfect surface for cutting on. It shows scratches (although they can be sanded out) and must be oiled frequently to maintain the finish and prevent water absorption.

Choosing countertop and backsplash materials

• **Heavy materials such as quartz, stone, and concrete** require strong bases.
• **Concrete and natural stone** are hard to fit and must be installed by a professional.
• **Poor heat resistance (such as thinner laminates and concrete)** means you need to have a hot pad or trivet available on which to place hot pans.
• **Poor scratch resistance (like tiles or steel)** requires you to use a chopping board or, better, have a butcher's block built in. Many people combine this with a built-in marble slab for rolling pasty. A pull-out chopping board is another option.
• **Flecked finishes with several colors** can be great for unifying the look of a room if they contain the other hues on the palette.

ACTION POINTS: using countertops and backsplashes

1 ENERGIZE WITH PATTERN. THE DISTINCTIVE DIAMOND-PATTERNED BLUE AND WHITE TILES ARE REFLECTED IN THE LUSTROUS SHINE OF A MARBLE COUNTERTOP.

2 ADD CONTRASTING TEXTURES. SLEEK BLUE MARBLE MAY NOT BE THE OBVIOUS CHOICE AS A COUNTERTOP, BUT HERE IT BALANCES THE HEAVY, RICH TEXTURES OF THE BEAMS, FLOOR, AND FIRE SURROUND.

3 SIMPLIFY THE LOOK. A SEMI-POLISHED BLUESTONE COUNTERTOP AND BACKSPLASH CREATE A UNIFIED BLOCK OF COLOR AND TEXTURE.

4 LIMIT COLORS FOR A SERENE LOOK. THE WHITES AND GRAYS OF MARBLE COMPLEMENT THE OTHER WHITE AND STAINLESS STEEL SURFACES IN THIS CONTEMPORARY KITCHEN.

The more cooking you do, the more sinks you need, so that food preparation doesn't clash with pot washing.

Sinks

The more cooking you do, the more sinks you need: really busy kitchens will have a triple-bowl sink for washing and rinsing pots and dishes, and a smaller sink for washing food, probably sited on an island—although remember this requires installing new drain lines and water supply lines. The key choices are material (see opposite), number and depth of bowls, and siting.

Considerations for your sinks are:
• **Location** Facing out or in from an island or peninsula?
• **Number of bowls** With two, you can soak encrusted baking trays in one and rinse dishes in the other. If space is at a premium, go for a one-and-a-half bowl, with the full bowl being longer than its width for roominess. A third, smaller, bowl is handy for washing salads.
• **Bowl depth** Older sinks have shallow bowls in which you can't soak big pots. Sinks are getting deeper.
• **Left- or right-handed?** A sink in which you'd expect to wash pots on the left, then rinse on the right, is known as a left-handed sink. You'll need a larger sink for washing than for rinsing.
• **Rounded corners** Easier to clean than square ones.
• **Mounting** Undermounting gives a seamless look and is easier to clean around. Drop-in sinks leave a raised rim that can trap dirt.

HERE, A PORCELAIN SINK IS UNDERMOUNTED BENEATH A LARGE SLAB OF BLACK MARBLE USED FOR THE COUNTERTOP. THE VINTAGE FAUCETS COMPLETE THE RUSTIC FARMHOUSE FINISH.

Material options

As with so many kitchen components, the more you study your options, the more choices you have, even over something as basic as what your sink will be made from.

Stainless steel has a timeless style and is extremely functional, being easy to clean and forgiving of dropped dishes—although it will scratch over time. It is kind to your budget, but there are still quality considerations. They come in various thicknesses. Thinner gauges can be noisy and the best option is often a thick gauge with a sound-dampening undercoating.

Enamelled cast iron or steel sinks are extremely durable and have the benefit of being made in bright colors, so they can suit retro and modern kitchen styles. Modern enamel is less prone to chipping than of old, but it will still wear over time and heavy pans may cause it to chip.

Composite sinks are made from acrylic resin and quartz compounds, which produce a speckled faux marble color and patterning. It is stain and dent resistant, but can be be hard to keep pristine.

Solid surface sinks come in a variety of colors and patterns, which form part of the material, so the surface won't chip or scratch. These stylish, attractive (and expensive) sinks can be part of the countertop for a modern seamless style. However, they don't cope with very hot pans and can stain.

ABOVE: SINKS CAN ADD VISUAL INTEREST, AS WITH THIS FARMHOUSE SINK SET UNDERNEATH THE MARBLE COUNTERTOP AND OVERHANGING THE TONGUE-AND-GROOVE CABINETRY, CREATING AN ARRAY OF INTERESTING LINES.

LEFT: STAINLESS STEEL SINKS ARE LIGHT REFLECTIVE AND DURABLE. WHEN TEAMED WITH CHROME FAUCETS AND STAINLESS STEEL APPLIANCES, THE END RESULT IS CHIC AND STREAMLINED.

A PULL-OUT FAUCET THAT CAN PROVIDE WATER OVER A WIDER AREA, FOR EXAMPLE INTO DOUBLE AND THREE-BOWL SINKS, IS HANDY. SOME PULL-OUTS DISPERSE WATER IN A STREAM OR A SPRAY, WHICH IS GREAT FOR RINSING AND WASHING.

Faucet options

choice	what	features
All-in-one faucet Single spout with a high swan neck. Separate controls for hot and cold water.	Elegant looks. Very good for filling pots. Suits modern-style kitchens but might look out of place in a period setting.
Deck-mounted faucet Bridge-pillar faucet with a two-hole feed. Separate controls for hot and cold water.	Simple and functional traditional look. Handles might restrict how far the spout can turn.
Single-lever faucet Also known as post-mount, operated from a side-mounted lever or top-mounted knob.	Easy to operate with dirty hands and offers very good temperature control, which is particularly important for children and the elderly.
Single-lever professional faucet All-in-one unit with controls at the spout end. Has a flexible hose (which can be pulled out) for washing and rinsing.	Particularly handy for use with two- or three-bowl sinks. Brings a hi-tech look to contemporary kitchens. Needs good water pressure, so may require a pump.
Traditional bib faucets with levers. Separate hot and cold faucets mounted side by side. The look is that of the nineteenth century.	Easy to use but with traditional styling, so suitable for period kitchens or for adding a quirky "retro" touch to the room. No mixing of temperatures.

Faucets

Faucets are one of the first things we tend to notice in the kitchen, and you want them to complement the style of the room. If you are installing new faucets you have an unusual opportunity to choose something that really complements the rest of the décor. For example, if you are looking for clean lines, can the faucet be mounted on the backsplash, giving the sink a neater edge? The most common faucet finish is chrome, which suits any kitchen and wipes clean, but there is a wealth of choices in finishes (polished, brushed), materials (enameled plastic, copper, gold, nickel, or brass), and colors and trims.

Beware of low spouts Remember that your pots, pans, and kettles must fit under the spout, which should also have sufficient reach to rinse all parts of the bowls in your sink. A pullout sprayer is handy for rinsing out pots and for washing vegetables.

Single or double controls? A single lever makes it easier to adjust the water temperature. This design also allows the spout to swing further, making work easier. If you prefer to turn on the faucets with the back of your hand or an elbow, levers are better than handles. A recent innovation is the pot-filler faucet, mounted on the wall behind the stove.

Instant hot-water dispenser This innovation means that you don't need to boil water when you want to make a hot drink—great if one person is around all day and likes to get a cup of tea or coffee with the minimum of fuss. Some people also have a soap dispenser fitted next to the spout.

Filtering faucet This option removes contaminants and odors, making your water more pleasant to drink. However, it wastes a lot of water in the process. If water quality is a really big issue in your household, you could go for a separate dedicated drinking water faucet with its own under-the-sink filter unit.

Garbage disposal While considering faucets and all things sink-related, you might want to consider installing one of these to allow you to get rid of food scraps and their smells quickly and easily. They grind waste into fine particles, which are then washed down the drain.

1 GOLD FAUCETS ADD A RICH LUSTER. IT IS IMPORTANT FOR FAUCETS TO MATCH OTHER MATERIALS IN THE KITCHEN.

2 A QUIRKY SPOUT SHAPE BRINGS CHARACTER. THE PULL-OUT SPRAYER ENSURES THE ARRANGEMENT IS PRACTICAL.

3 THE LEVERS ON THIS DECK-MOUNTED FAUCET ARE PRACTICAL AND FUNCTIONAL, MATCHING MOST KITCHEN STYLES.

Appliances

Choosing kitchen appliances is a big shopping opportunity where the options seem just about endless. Do consider your overall look (colors, facings, kitchen style) with each choice, but of course the top criteria has to be whether the appliance does a good job at meeting your needs.

It is very easy to be tempted by low-price appliances—and there are times when there are bargains to be had as manufacturers try to move last year's stock. However, it is worth considering the operating costs and the price of repairs and maintenance. An energy-efficient appliance with a record of reliability is worth more than a cheaper one without these attributes.

Cooking appliances

The choice of cooking appliances is so wide you have to be ruthless in eliminating the options that won't suit you (however great they look).

The key question is: What sort of cooking do you do? If you feed a large family or do lots of entertaining, a large freestanding range offers the capacity you need for multiple dishes and includes features such as warming drawers. If your needs are smaller scale, an oven with a cooktop will suffice. If two cooks are likely to work simultaneously, a wall oven with a separate cooktop will help avoid competition for space. If healthy meals are a priority, maybe you need an additional steam oven to produce food without oils or sauces. A really keen baker may need two ovens, or at least one with a larger capacity. A steak-loving family might enjoy a built-in grill.

The other important consideration is whether you already know where the stove will go. This will determine whether you have built-in or freestanding appliances. If it is in a large central space like a recess, a wide range will provide a focal point (they dominate wherever you put them). A large, enamel-coated, European-style stove really suits a big, country-style kitchen. If the overall look is to be streamlined, a wall-mounted oven is suitable. If you want to cook on an island, it will require electrical supply and an exhaust hood. If you cook on gas, the range location may be decided by the supply source.

The key features of cooking appliances include:
• **The finish** Contrast with or match other features.
• **Fuel** Gas is easier to control; electricity produces a drier heat; duel-fuel ovens use both.
• **Ease of cleaning** Many ovens have self-cleaning systems of varying effectiveness. The door should also be easy to clean. With cooktops, the smoother the finish, the

easier it is to clean. Finishes such as stainless steel look great but can become a canvas for handfuls of greasy fingerprints, which are hard to remove.

• **Front-mounted controls** keep hands further away from the heat.

• **Safety features,** such as control locks and hot-surface indicators.

• **Energy efficiency.**

Choosing a range The standard width of a range is 30 inches, but many are 36 inches and professional-style ranges that look similar to restaurant equipment can go up to double that figure. Their styles vary, from the stainless steel industrial look to those that try to blend in through the use of smooth lines and integrated panels. Larger ranges tend to dominate the room. Bigger models are often deeper than standard cabinet depth, so will jut out slightly.

Choosing an oven Conventional ovens use gas or electricity to radiate heat in the space. Convection ovens are electric and have a fan to circulate the hot air, reducing cooking times and spreading the heat more evenly. Many units have a large convection oven and a smaller oven together with a broiler. The capacity varies with the model, but check that the oven you select accommodates your cookie sheets and roasting pans.

BELOW: BUSY COOKS NEED MORE EQUIPMENT. HERE A RANGE SITS NEXT TO A MATCHING WALL-MOUNTED OVEN.

BELOW RIGHT: THIS ARRANGEMENT IS SIMILAR, BUT THE BLACK FINISH OF THE OVEN PICKS UP THE DARK HUE OF THE WOODEN FLOOR.

OPPOSITE: BY CHOOSING AN EXHAUST HOOD THAT DOESN'T FALL TOO LOW, THERE IS SPACE ABOVE THE STOVE FOR A SHELF FOR STORING SPICES AND COOKING UTENSILS.

A separate oven can be installed higher up on a wall, making it easier to place and remove the food. This is valuable if anyone has a back problem or if you cook a lot of heavy roasts. Such a location suits modern, streamlined kitchens.

Choosing a cooktop The standard cooktop has four gas or electric burners: larger models have six. Gas-fueled cooktops may have two high-heat rapid burners and two simmer burners. Standard electric burners heat up slowly, but there may be halogen burners that perform faster.The cooktop needs to suit your style of cooking: if you boil or steam lots of vegetables while preparing a sauce, you need more burners than if you tend to cook casseroles where all the ingredients are in one container.

Choosing an exhaust hood A key consideration of kitchen planning is disposing of the heat, steam, and grease that is inevitably produced. The usual method is via an exhaust hood, which is a unit housed over the cooktop and pumps air out of the room through the wall or roof. Cooktops on islands might need a more complicated system.

Choosing a microwave These have become kitchen mainstays. The speed of microwave cooking means they generate a lot of traffic when in use. They are best installed in a cabinet space at waist or head height.

A separate oven installed higher up on a wall can be valuable if anyone using it has a back problem or likes to cook a lot of heavy roasts.

Refrigerators

The major choice is the finish: blending in with white or off-white or wood, matching metal appliances with stainless steel, or making a big statement with a strong color—perfect for a retro kitchen. Built-in fridges will be concealed behind doors that match the cabinetry, but cost significantly more than the freestanding variety.

The refrigerator needs to match your lifestyle, too: small households need less chilled storage space than a large family. Those with a great thirst for iced and chilled water will enjoy a through-the-door dispenser (which can also be energy-saving). There is a growing trend toward having dedicated wine and beer coolers in the kitchen or the pantry. Another important consideration is configuration (see below).

Other points to bear in mind are:
• **All new refrigerators must display an energy rating** showing their efficiency, and the best performers have the Energy Star logo. This is significant as the refrigerator is the single biggest power consumer in most households.
• **If you purchase a lot of frozen food,** or freeze leftovers, you could opt for a separate and larger freezer for bulk storage, which could be located in the basement or an outbuilding.
• **A small second fridge for wine,** other beverages, or a built-in refrigerated drawer give you more chilled storage.
• **Be clear about where the hinge should be.** If you pile up groceries to the right of the fridge, you don't want to have to walk round a right-hinged door to stack them.
• **Removable shelves** are easier to wash.
• **The motors and self-defrosting mechanisms of fridges can be noisy,** which can be very irritating if your kitchen is as quiet as a library. Ask to hear them working in the store.
• **Configurations vary.** Those with the freezer over the refrigerator allow easy access to chilled items for children and the elderly, but frequently reaching down for low items may be hard on your back, and the ice cubes may be out of reach. Refrigerator over freezer layouts are easy to clean and for adults to use. Side-by-sides can be very narrow, so consider whether your party platters will fit.

ABOVE: A FREESTANDING ICE MAKER IS A POPULAR CHOICE FOR FAMILIES WHO LIKE THEIR BEVERAGES WELL CHILLED.

OPPOSITE: BIG REFRIGERATORS MAKE BIG DESIGN STATEMENTS. THE INDUSTRIAL-STYLE STAINLESS STEEL OF THIS ONE CONTRASTS WITH OLD FASHIONED WOODEN DOOR AND CHAIRS. WITH THE OVERSIZED REFRIGERATING COMPARTMENTS, ITS CONTENTS CAN BE PLENTIFUL AND WELL ORGANIZED.

Dishwashers

This kitchen essential can be hidden behind panels matching its neighboring cabinets. The dishwasher is ideally located between the sink and where dishes are stored, possibly at a raised level for easier loading and unloading, preferably on the same wall as the sink for ease of plumbing. Dishwashers carry an energy rating, and can vary in capacity to suit smaller or more frequent loads. If people like to sit and chat in the kitchen, the noise of this machine can be very distracting, so you may wish to seek dishwashers with quiet motors and good insulation.

Electrical equipment

You should have a pretty good idea of where you are likely to use toasters, blenders, food processors, and any other electrical equipment. You want to make sure there is an electrical outlet conveniently situated for you to plug it in. Outlets detract from the décor. You may be able to find covers that blend (perhaps stainless steel). You could fit the outlet inside a cabinet so that it is kept hidden away, enhancing the look of your kitchen. Kitchens are power-hungry places, so always have double outlets installed and add as many as you can when the electrician is around!

Although they aren't used for food preparation, computer centers and stereo and TV equipment are all finding favor in the kitchen. This is very much a lifestyle decision but if planned from the start, such equipment can be fitted into kitchen-style cabinets so that the feel of the room is kept consistent.

SOMETIMES APPLIANCES STICK OUT LIKE A SORE THUMB, BUT MATCHING ELECTRICAL APPLIANCES LIKE THIS STAINLESS STEEL BLENDER AND TOASTER ARE PERFECTLY AT HOME IN THE RIGHT DECORATIVE ENVIRONMENT.

ACTION POINTS: using appliances

1 KEEP A CLEAR WORK SPACE. A COFFEEMAKER AND TOASTER NESTLE TOWARD THE BACK OF THE COUNTERTOP LEAVING SUFFICIENT SPACE IN FRONT FOR RESTING CUPS FOR THE COFFEE AND PLATES FOR THE TOAST.

2 USE NATURAL MATERIALS FOR WARMTH. COMBINING STAINLESS STEEL APPLIANCES WITH MAHOGONY UNITS AND SOFT BROWN TILES BRINGS A WELCOMING WARMTH TO THE CLEAN AND CONTEMPORARY LOOK.

3 PLAN FOR COUNTER SPACE NEAR THE STOVE. WHEN POSITIONING YOUR STOVE, ENSURE THERE IS SUFFICIENT COUNTERTOP NEARBY FOR PREPARATION AND PRESENTATION.

4 HAVE ENOUGH COLD STORAGE. DEEP AND WIDE STAINLESS STEEL COMMERCIAL REFRIGERATORS HAVE TAKEN THE MARKET BY STORM.

storage

Storage is a vital element in kitchen design because you've got to keep equipment and ingredients somewhere within easy reach. How these small items are concealed or displayed goes a long way to setting the overall kitchen style. The spectrum ranges from the rustic look of open wooden shelves, where everything is on show, to the minimalist modern look, where all the clutter is concealed behind doors leaving only a few stylish items on display.

You need to plan for as much storage space as possible. Even if you don't think you'll fill it, you will—and over the years you will acquire more equipment and utensils that make life at the stove easier and more enjoyable. It's all got to live somewhere!

We all have a storage style: some of us are happy living alongside piles of familiar, cozy clutter, which to others is just a stress-inducing mound of "things to do." Some kitchens have a way of attracting clutter and becoming a mish-mash of food, utensils, recipe books, magazines, cell phones, and little families of unclassifiable objects huddled on the edge of a shelf.

Your kitchen storage style will be dictated by how you view clutter and your overall kitchen style: a country-kitchen table doesn't look right bare—it is crying out for a mixing bowl and a half-cut loaf of bread resting on a wooden board; while the same things look completely out of place in the middle of a minimalist kitchen, where clean lines are important and such items are kept hidden away.

When planning your storage, decide carefully what will go where, thinking about logic and convenience. Pots and pans must be near the stove or cooktop, and coffee and spices should be kept out of the light because they deteriorate when exposed to it for long periods. For convenience, store fruit and vegetables near the prep area.

ABOVE: CLEARLY VISIBLE NEAT PILES OF WHITE DISHES ADD VISUAL INTEREST WITHOUT INTRUDING INTO THIS SMALL, WHITE KITCHEN.

OPPOSITE: GLASS-FRONTED CABINETS ALLOW YOU TO DISPLAY INTERESTING DISHES WHILE KEEPING THEM CLEAN. NOTICE HOW THE BACKGROUNDS OF THE TOP CABINETS HAVE BEEN PAINTED AN ASSORTMENT OF BRIGHT COLORS, PERFECTLY OFFSETTING THE WHITE PLATES IN FRONT.

Anything used very occasionally (for instance, a seasonally decorated platter on which you serve the Thanksgiving turkey) can be placed high up on top of a wall cabinet. If some appliances detract from the kitchen style and aren't used every day, store them out of sight rather than displaying them on a countertop or shelf.

Built-in or freestanding?

Built-in cabinets are by far the neatest way of providing storage just where you need it, under a countertop. Add matching wall-mounted cabinets above the work surface and you've gone a long way to meeting your storage needs. But the effect is very uniform and lacks individuality. You might choose to use some stand-alone cupboards or a sideboard for variety (in a painted kitchen, you can make them match the other cabinets with a few brush strokes). This also gives some height variation, bringing a bit of character and making the kitchen more interesting to the eye.

A traditional sideboard looks great with its neat displays of dishes and is still often the best solution in limited space or as an addition to a set of ready-made cabinets.

Shelves Your decision on kitchen style is likely to determine how much open shelving you want, if any. The great thing about shelves is that they can be made to fit any

The most useful storage level is from knee to shoulder height, so store your most frequently used items within this band.

space and can look attractive in their own right. The downsides are that they display their contents and gather dust. They are therefore best for storing items that are used reasonably frequently, such as dishes, glassware, and cooking pots. Heavy items require strong supports. Shelves are the ideal place for cookbooks, which need to be within easy reach to help solve that crisis moment when you realize you haven't got a key ingredient and you need a quick substitute.

Wood, plywood, medium density fiberboard (MDF), and glass are all fine materials for shelving. Although you can go for adjustable shelves, you are unlikely to want to change the levels once they are in place, and fixed shelving is far more attractive.

Racks Hanging racks mounted on the wall or ceiling are a fine way to store cooking utensils and equipment right where they will be used and fit in with most kitchen styles. They have a pleasing, down-to-earth feel and never seem cluttered in the way a shelf or cabinet can.

Islands Aim to keep the top of the island empty so that sight lines are not disturbed. However, a built-in cupboard under an island countertop can offer extra storage space, especially for equipment that will be used on the island itself. If you want to use the island for display, look for a unit with open shelves.

OPPOSITE: THIS BRIGHTLY COLORED CHINAWARE IS USED TO MAXIMUM EFFECT BY SHOWING IT OFF ON OPEN SHELVES.

BELOW LEFT: IF OPEN SHELVES AREN'T TO YOUR TASTE, BUT YOU HAVE PRETTY GLASS TO DISPLAY, CHOOSE GLASS-FRONTED CABINETS INSTEAD.

BELOW: THIS ANTIQUE SET OF SHELVES HAS BEEN USED FOR CHINA AND DISPLAYING FAVORITE OBJECTS, BUT IT COULD EQUALLY BE USED FOR MORE PRACTICAL STORAGE.

ACTION POINTS: using shelves and racks

1 SHOW IT OFF. GLASS-FRONTED UNITS ADD DEPTH IN THIS LOVELY KITCHEN.

2 MAKE A PRETTY DISPLAY. OPEN SHELVES LOOK COZIER AND MEAN THAT EVERYTHING IS WITHIN EASY REACH.

3 HANG IT UP. BY INSTALLING A RACK THAT RUNS THE FULL LENGTH OF THE COUNTERTOP, YOU CAN HANG SUCH THINGS AS SPICE RACKS ABOVE YOUR WORK AREA.

4 BE READY TO COOK. AS WELL AS BEING FUNCTIONAL, POTS HUNG ON RACKS CAN LOOK GREAT, ESPECIALLY WHEN THEY MATCH THE RANGE UNDERNEATH.

GLASS-FRONTED CABINETS MAKE A ROOM SEEM BIGGER AND BRIGHTER BY ADDING DEPTH AND REFLECTING LIGHT. BY PAINTING THE CABINET WHITE AND FILLING IT ONLY WITH WHITE DISHES AND CRYSTAL GLASS, THE FINISHED EFFECT IS BOTH SOPHISTICATED AND UNDERSTATED.

Cabinets

New cabinetry often accounts for about half the total kitchen renovation budget. Cabinets can be constructed solely in wood, or in particleboard, plywood, or medium density fiberboard (MDF). Well-built cases cost more but will last far longer, possibly offering the option of refreshing the kitchen in due course by simply repainting or, if the style is dated or they are showing signs of wear, replacing the doors.

You have a choice of stock, semi-custom, or custom cabinets:
• **Stock cabinets** Ready-made laminate cabinets sold through home centers. They are available in a range of styles and standard sizes and are easily installed by a competent do-it-yourselfer, although filler strips may be required to cover any gaps. Stock cabinets are usually the cheapest option but it is always worth checking the quality before you buy them.
• **Semi-custom cabinets** Stock cabinets with modifications, such as pullout bins or other specifications. They are factory-made to your specifications and measurements.
• **Custom cabinets** Made in hardwood to fit by a carpenter. They are stronger than stock cabinets and can be expensive, but much depends on the style and materials selected. Custom cabinets are often the only option for an oddly shaped kitchen.
In addition to the way a cabinet is manufactured, there are either the traditional face-

Face-frame vs frameless cabinets

choice	what	features
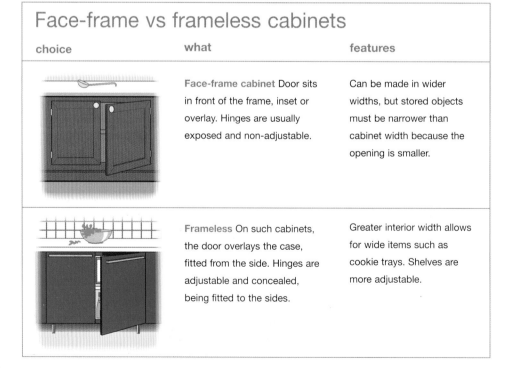	**Face-frame cabinet** Door sits in front of the frame, inset or overlay. Hinges are usually exposed and non-adjustable.	Can be made in wider widths, but stored objects must be narrower than cabinet width because the opening is smaller.
	Frameless On such cabinets, the door overlays the case, fitted from the side. Hinges are adjustable and concealed, being fitted to the sides.	Greater interior width allows for wide items such as cookie trays. Shelves are more adjustable.

frame or the European-influenced (and slightly more expensive) frameless type to decide between (see opposite, below).

Think through cabinet placement and especially heights carefully: a short cook needs lower cabinets! Varying the cabinet height can add visual interest and if the counter levels vary, the cabinet heights should match to keep the look consistent.

Tops and bottoms

Floor-to-ceiling cabinets have a large capacity and so are particularly valuable in small kitchens. The smaller the space between cabinet top and ceiling, the less room there is for dust and dirt to collect, but leaving a space above a cabinet makes the room seem more airy. An alternative is to finish it off with a deep crown molding. Toe-kicks are also good dirt-deterers, but placing cabinets on legs gives the impression that the furniture is floating above the floor, adding to the sense of depth in the room. A pullout cabinet open on both sides offers masses of storage with easy access—great for storing all your cans and bags of flour because you can remove them from either side. Such a cabinet is available either as full height or an under-countertop version (see picture 4 on page 85).

Today's cabinets are more versatile than ever: they needn't all look exactly the same if you don't want them to.

PLATE RACKS OFFER ATTRACTIVE AND PRACTICAL STORAGE, PARTICULARLY HERE WHERE THEY ARE SITED SYMMETRICALLY ON EITHER SIDE OF THE SINK.

Doors and drawers

FACE-FRAME DOORS ADD DEPTH
TO BALANCE THE FLAT SURFACES
OF THE STAINLESS STEEL
APPLIANCES AND COUNTERTOPS.

Your choice of door style will have an enormous impact on how your kitchen looks because doors occupy such a large area at or just below eye level. Plain, unadorned doors can look stylish but their uniformity can seem monotonous. Molding or inlay on

doors attracts the eye, but it also traps dirt. If your existing cabinets are in good condition, you could save a lot of time and money by repainting or refacing them. Wooden doors can be painted or stained very easily. They'll need to be thoroughly smoothed with fine grit sandpaper, cleaned, and (for painting) primed. However, if the doors and drawer fronts are very worn or no longer suit your style, they can be replaced in any style you wish through refacing. Most home centers will be able to

door styles

choice	what	features
	Clear glass in a wood or metal frame.	Expensive. Excellent for displaying dishes and glasses and for seeing where things are stored. Can't take abrasive cleaners and can be hard to keep pristine.
	Frosted or patterned glass in a wood or metal frame.	Works well with interior lighting inside the cabinet, but can seem a little cold. The contents do not have to be kept so tidy.
	Solid wood This has a stylish appearance. The doors can be left natural or painted.	Interior stays dark, so good for storing light-sensitive foods, such as spices and coffee. If there is a row of such cabinets, they can look overly uniform.
	Wire mesh in a wooden frame.	Adds depth and brings a rustic touch. Allows for display of dishes, which must be kept neat. Dust can gather inside the cabinet.

order the necessary materials for you and the installation is a relatively simple job—or you can ask a carpenter to do it. Whether you are refacing or buying whole new units, you have a choice of door and drawer-front styles and materials (see below).

Drawers Doweled or dovetailed joints are a sign of top drawer quality (as opposed to those that are stapled and glued). Good weight-bearing full-extension drawer glides allow you to pull the drawer all the way out, making it easier to use, as items stored at the back won't get lost. Try the drawers at the showroom, looking for wobbles and sticking. Check out how noisy the glides are in action: those with ball bearings rather than nylon rollers are easier on the ears. Soft-action glides slow to a crawl a couple of inches out so that fingers can't get trapped. Pullouts (which are drawers hidden behind the cabinet doors) are usually shallow, good for cookie sheets and pizza trays.

If there is room for a drawer under the oven, this is the spot for pots and pans. Households with pets such as cats and dogs may be interested in having pullout drawers with feeding bowls.

Cabinet hardware

It is easy to start feeling rather punch-drunk by this stage as you have been making decision after decision, but this is your chance to make your kitchen truly individual and to add some valuable safety and convenience features.

Hinges These may be decorative, concealed, or semiconcealed. A useful option for high cabinets is a mechanism that glides up, away from your head. Double-fold doors also reduce the chances of head banging.

Handles and pulls Your choice of door handles and pulls offers an opportunity to add some kitchen character, from hiding them altogether to adding an intricate design in weathered bronze. Possible materials include wood, metal (such as brushed nickel, brass, or stainless steel), ceramic, glass, and plastic. Do test your choices as some pulls can look great but are clumsy to use. Replacing the handles is a great, inexpensive way to carry out a quick image change, and worth bearing in mind after a few years: these fittings can date faster than anything else in the kitchen.

ABOVE: SCALLOPED WOODWORK DETAILING AND THE ECHOING CURVES OF THE CABINET HINGES ADD CHARM TO THIS CORNER.

OPPOSITE: THE INLAID DRAWERS, DOORS, AND CERAMIC KNOBS OF THESE CABINETS AND DRAWERS CREATE AN INTERESTING AND PLEASING DECORATIVE PATTERN.

ACTION POINTS: door handles

1 CONSIDER A MINIMAL STYLE. CIRCULAR HOLES CUT INTO WOOD MAKE PRACTICAL HANDLES THAT FORM INTERESTING PATTERNS WITHOUT BREAKING UP THE LINES OF THIS ROOM.

2 MAKE A DESIGN STATEMENT. THESE CLASSIC TUBULAR HANDLES ARE SLEEK AND FUNCTIONAL, THEIR METAL ECHOING THE STAINLESS STEEL OF THE COOKER AND REFRIGERATOR.

3 MIX IT UP. HANDLES DON'T HAVE TO MATCH: SIMPLE PLASTIC KNOBS MATCH THE BOLD TILES OF THE BACKSPLASH, WHILE THE METAL CURVES ON THE DRAWERS SOFTEN THE LINE OF THE UNIT IN FRONT.

4 SIMPLIFY FOR AN UNCLUTTERED EFFECT. IF THE SURFACES AND SHELVES ARE CLUTTERED, GO FOR THE SIMPLEST POSSIBLE HANDLES SO THAT THE OVERALL FEEL IS NOT TOO "BUSY."

Storage accessories

You can never have too much kitchen storage and exploring the options goes way beyond having plenty of cabinets: you have many ways to make the most of the storage space available. These are well worth investigating because clever devices can make traditionally "lost" space, such as corners, more productive (see opposite).

Storage accessory options

choice	what	benefits
	Accessories for corner cabinets, such as swing-out racks or lazy Susans.	The hard-to-reach dark interiors of corner cabinets can be a kitchen graveyard. These systems offer easy access to every square inch.
	Hanging pot rack either mounted on the wall or hanging from the ceiling over an island or close to the stove.	Looks great and allows storage of pots and pans close to where they will be used. Also makes a decorative feature of attractive shiny finishes.
	Internal dividers to create compartments inside drawers, allowing easy storage of small items.	Have some fitted next to the stove and you'll always have the right utensil or a dry towel at hand.
	Knife racks or knife drawers for safe storage of sharp blades.	Blades are quickly blunted by contact with other objects when stored in a jumble. A knife rack looks attractive and ensures you've got your knives safely stored.
	Racks on the backs of doors turn a wasted space into an extra storage place where every item is easily seen and reached.	This allows easy storage of frequently used items such as condiments and spices.

Trash talk

Kitchens generate a lot of trash, from food packaging to fruit peelings, and in these environment-conscious days any kitchen should be geared to recycling as much as possible. It is easier to plan this from the start rather than adding it later. Some ideas are:

- *A pullout bin beneath your prep area lets you brush away peelings instantly.*

- *A storage cabinet for recycling containers such as cans or bottles, possibly in the pantry or mudroom.*

- *Installing a trash compactor to reduce the bulk of the garbage leaving your house.*

OPPOSITE: DON'T BE AFRAID TO IMPROVISE TO IMPROVE STORAGE. HERE WIRE BASKETS HAVE BEEN PLACED ON THE LOWER SHELVES OF A WOODEN UNIT, WHICH HAS BEEN CLEVERLY ADAPTED WITH A MARBLE TOP AND THE ADDITION OF TWO SINKS.

ACTION POINTS: using storage accessories

1 DIVIDE AND CONQUER. A FLATWARE ORGANIZER KEEPS ALL THOSE UTENSILS AND GADGETS IN THE RIGHT PLACE.

2 RETHINK YOUR DRAWERS. ADJUSTABLE POSTS THAT CAN BE SLOTTED INTO ANY HOLE IN THE BASE CREATE A SET OF DIVIDERS ALLOWING STORAGE OF PILES OF DISHES WITHOUT THE RISK OF THEM CHIPPING.

3 SAVE YOUR BACK. KEEPING SAUCEPANS IN PULL-OUT DRAWERS MEANS THAT YOU CAN STORE THEM AT A CONVENIENT HEIGHT CLOSE TO WHERE THEY WILL BE USED.

4 USE EVERY INCH. A UNIT OF SHELVES THAT SLIDES OUT MAKES THE MOST OF NARROW SPACES AND IS PERFECT FOR STORING HERBS AND SPICES, AMONG OTHER THINGS.

floors

ABOVE: STONE TILES LAID AT AN
ANGLE TO THE WALLS ADD A
PLEASING TOUCH OF ASYMMETRY
TO THIS CALIFORNIA KITCHEN.

OPPOSITE: FLOOR SHOW! THE
STRIKING DEEP BLUE OF THIS
GLAZED CERAMIC-TILED FLOOR
IS REFLECTED IN THE STAINLESS
STEEL APPLIANCES TO GREAT
DRAMATIC EFFECT.

The kitchen floor is the hardest-working surface in your home. It has to cope with heavy traffic, moisture, and all kinds of oily, fatty, acidic spills—and you want it to look great too! Choosing flooring material is a decision that juggles durability with looks, maintenance, and cost, including that of installation.

One material you can cross straight off the list is carpeting: it is completely unsuitable for kitchen environments because it can't cope with the spills that are inevitable where food is prepared and eaten. That's the easy part. Many choices remain, all suitable for this role, so it makes sense to consider the look you want and how it will complement the rest of the décor. The options break down into three categories: ceramic and stone, wood, and resilient flooring materials, such as vinyl.

One factor you might wish to consider is your local environment: if you live among trees, a wooden floor would seem more suitable than vinyl, for example, while in a rocky setting the sliced-up boulders of a stone floor will feel at home. If you are installing thick flooring materials, such as solid wood or stone, the floor level will rise slightly: do check that doors will still open over it!

Ceramic tiles (see overleaf) offer a medium-cost, highly durable option with a massive choice of colors, patterns, and textures, so you can match or complement the finish of your countertop or backsplash. Alternatively, a stone floor can look really striking and a range of finishes is available (see page 89). Wood (see pages 92–95) is a warm and inviting finish but can have its drawbacks in the damp environment of a kitchen, in which case you might want to consider one of the wide range of resilient floorings that are available (see pages 96–99).

THE BLUES AND WHITES IN THIS
TILED FLOOR DRAW THE EYE
AROUND THE ROOM AND ECHO
THE TEXTURE OF THE MARBLE
COUNTERTOP. BY USING CERAMIC
OR GLASS TILES IT IS JUST AS
SIMPLE TO CREATE A PATTERNED
FLOOR AS ONE THAT IS MADE OF
A SINGLE COLOR.

Ceramic floors

There are many ceramic tiles to choose from, each with different characteristics (see below). They can be cheap compared to stone, but prices vary widely. They are very easy to maintain. Ceramic floors can, however, feel cold and become slippery when wet. As with stone, breakable items falling onto this material are likely to shatter—and some tiles chip easily, too. Beware, too, the grouting can stain and discolor.

Glass and ceramic floor tile options

choice	what	features
	Glass tiles Available in a huge range of sizes, shapes, colors, and finishes—here panels are shown laid in a parquet-like style. They are impervious to water and can be treated to be slip resistant.	Glass tiles can create a stunning floor because of their luminescence, texture, and color. They are highly reflective, maximizing the light in a room.
	Glazed tiles Machine-made clay tiles, available in many colors. Finishes can be glossy or matte.	Durability varies. The glaze resists water, but unglazed edges do not.
	Porcelain tiles Made from highly refined clay and usually come in an earth tone. They can be glazed or unglazed.	Highly durable and moisture resistant.
	Quarry tiles Terra-cotta tiles have an attractive, earthy appearance.	These have lower durability than porcelain and require regular resealing.

Stone floors

If the budget allows for it, stone is the classic kitchen flooring material because it looks great and is virtually indestructible. However, stone floors require more maintenance than ceramic tiles, and can feel unwelcomingly cold underfoot (underfloor radiant heating cures this deficiency, at a price). Like tiles, stone is unforgiving of dropped items such as glasses and bowls.

Stone floor options

choice	what	features
	Granite Formed from molten rock, this is a very hard stone (almost as tough as a diamond) with interesting veined patterns. It is available in various colors.	Highly durable and virtually impervious to water. It does not scratch but can stain easily. Can be polished to a high-gloss finish.
	Marble Has the widest variety of colors and textures and with its delicate veining is often seen as the most beautiful stone.	Must be sealed to stave off dirt, scratches, and stains. Can be slippery when polished or wet.
	Manufactured stone Also known as engineered stone, this is an artificial stone made by mixing pieces of quartz with resin.	Does not scratch or stain easily. Easy to maintain. It comes in a range of colors and finishes so can match many kitchen styles.
	Slate Can be gray, blue, green, or black, and is great for the rustic look as it comes in irregular shapes.	Slate must be sealed as it can stain and scratch easily. It is very hardwearing, and the least expensive real stone option.

THE ZINC-TOPPED ISLAND COUNTERTOP IS MATCHED BY THE BEAUTIFUL BLUE/GRAY STONE FLOOR TILES. THE DARK GRAY GROUTING EMPHASIZES THE GENEROUS SIZE OF THE TILES.

ACTION POINTS: ceramic and stone floors

1 TRY TERRA-COTTA FOR A WARM LOOK. THIS IS THE MOST INVITING OF THE CERAMIC FINISHES, ADDING TO THE COZY CHARM OF THIS KITCHEN.

2 TIE IT TOGETHER WITH TILES. ANTIQUE BRICK-SHAPED TILES HAVE BEEN USED FOR THE FLOOR AND BACKSPLASH IN THIS WELL-PROPORTIONED RUSTIC-STYLE ROOM.

3 ENTERTAIN THE EYE WITH PATTERN. A KEY BENEFIT OF STONE AND CERAMIC TILES IS THAT THEY CAN BE CUT TO ANY SHAPE. HERE THE HEXAGONS MAKE A PLEASING PATTERN.

4 MAKE IT MARBLE FOR CLASSIC STYLE. THE COOL STYLE OF THIS MARBLE FLOOR IS PERFECTLY SUITED TO THE SMOOTH CONTEMPORARY LINES OF ITS SETTING.

Wood

Nothing beats wood for warmth and beauty. A solid wood floor (usually hardwoods such as oak, maple, or cherry, but sometimes pine, which is a softwood) is comprised of strips or planks nailed down, sometimes stained, and sealed. Wood is a very popular choice because in addition to looking wonderful it can match kitchen materials or trim. For wooden floors in high traffic areas like kitchens, get the floor treated with a penetrating sealer like polyurethane so that it can just be swept and mopped. This can be done after installation or at the factory.

However, even sealed wood doesn't like the wet: spills need to be wiped up promptly to avoid staining, and a bad leak from a washing machine or dishwasher could result in a stained and possibly warped floor. Wood will gather dents and scratches over time (and it really hates high heels). Most people regard this as part of the patina of life, but if you want to avoid it, consider a synthetic wood (see below). Don't forget too, that all real wood darkens as it ages, especially when exposed to sunlight.

Synthetic woods A cheaper option is engineered wood, which is plywood with a thin layer of real wood glued to the top. Synthetic flooring is durable and stain- and scratch-resistant, but if it does get damaged, you'll need to replace a section of floor. Another choice is laminate flooring, which has a photographic image (which can be anything, but is usually wood) attached to a fiberboard backing layer.

BELOW: THE INTRICATE PATTERNS OF PARQUET FLOORING OFFSET THE COOL MINIMALISM OF THE REST OF THIS ROOM.

BELOW RIGHT: THE SIMPLE EXPEDIENT OF PAINTING THE KITCHEN FLOORBOARDS WHITE MARKS THE DIVIDE BETWEEN LIVING SPACE AND KITCHEN WITHOUT HINDERING THE FLOW BETWEEN ROOMS.

wood options

choice		what	features
		Bamboo	Laminated into planks, bamboo exudes warmth and is as attractive as wood. It is stronger than many natural woods such as oak.
		Beech	Fine-grained with a pale pinkish brown tint. Very durable and heavy. Not suitable for staining.
		Maple	Has a subtle, fine grain and a rich, consistent color. Particularly suits a clean, contemporary look.
		Oak	Has a characterful, pronounced grain and is often used for kitchen floors. Available in white and (warmer) red varieties.
		Pine	Pale yellow tones look best in rustic-style kitchens in period homes. As a softwood, it dents easily. Not suitable for staining.
		Synthetic wood	Durable and copes well in kitchen environments: a good low-budget option but without the character of solid wood.

THIS FLOOR IS RECOGNIZABLY WOODEN, LIKE THE CABINETS, BUT THE STRIKING COBALT-BLUE STAIN ADDS AN AIR OF COOL SOPHISTICATION.

ACTION POINTS: using wood floors

1 STICK WITH TRADITION.
AN INTRICATELY DESIGNED
AND LAID WOODEN FLOOR IS A
FINE PLATFORM FOR THE
NINETEENTH-CENTURY AMERICAN
FRUITWOOD FURNITURE.

2 TIE IT TOGETHER WITH
COLOR. PAINTING THIS
WOODEN FLOOR WITH DIAMOND
SHAPES IN THE SAME BLUE-GRAY
SHADE AS THE CUPBOARD
SUCCESSFULLY LINKS THE TWO
ELEMENTS.

3 COMBINE NATURE'S
MATERIALS. WOOD AND
WICKER ARE NATURAL PARTNERS,
AS SHOWN WITH THE FLOOR,
ISLAND, COUNTERTOP,
AND CHAIRS HERE.

4 VARY THE STAINS FOR
CONTRAST. DIFFERENT
SHADES OF WOOD USED FOR
THE TALL CABINET AND FLOOR
BRING GRAVITAS TO THIS LIGHT
COUNTRY KITCHEN.

Resilient flooring

Resilient flooring is so-called because it is slightly cushioned and so bounces back to retain its shape. The main types are linoleum and vinyl. These have long been popular choices for kitchen flooring because they are inexpensive, very easy to maintain, highly durable, and cope effortlessly with the spills, stains, and scuffs of kitchen life. They come in a wide range of colors to complement almost any decorative scheme.

Cork flooring is an environmentally sound choice because it is a renewable resource, harvested from the bark of a type of oak tree that grows mainly in Spain and Portugal. Cork has excellent sound insulation qualities, which make it a good choice in apartments and in high-ceiling rooms where sound can reverberate.

Linoleum Made from natural materials, linoleum is made from felt or canvas coated with linseed oil, cork, and resins. It is available in sheet form, lasts forever, and comes in any color. Linoleum is the perfect flooring material for retro kitchens and its practicality makes it top choice for hard-working, less public areas like mudrooms.

Rubber A long-time favorite in health-care, restaurant, and other commercial settings, rubber flooring is slip-resistant, durable, and its cushioned texture makes it kind to knees and backs. Rubber is easy to clean and copes happily with grease and liquid spills. The material is natural and can be made from recycled tires. Rubber also has good sound absorbency so could be a good choice in a high-ceilinged room where sound echoes around. It is available in textured sheets or tiles. Rubber flooring is long lasting and the many bright colors won't fade.

Vinyl This inexpensive, plastic material is available in sheet or tile form, and is highly popular because of the vast range of colors, designs, and textures offered, together with its ease of maintenance (so it is particularly good for family kitchens). Sheet vinyl can be cut in to any shape, so it is also a good choice for a room with odd dimensions. Vinyl tiles aren't always the best option for kitchens. After repeated exposure to heavy traffic and kitchen moisture, every seam will show.

1 VINTAGE BLACK AND WHITE TILES ARE A CLASSIC KITCHEN FLOOR, ADDING INTEREST TO THE WHITE COLOR SCHEME.

2 A LINOLEUM STRIPE ELONGATES THIS SMALL, NARROW KITCHEN AND FOCUSES ATTENTION ON THE WINDOW.

3 THE RED VINYL FLOOR PLAYS A MAJOR PART IN KEEPING THIS UTILITY ROOM BRIGHT AND CHEERFUL.

Resilient flooring options

choice	what	features
	Cork Essentially these are vinyl tiles but with an added decorative layer made from cork.	Soft under foot and so kind to the cook's knees. It also has excellent insulation qualities.
	Linoleum Made from natural materials and comes in a wide range of colors and finishes.	Slip, scratch, and dent resistant. Can be noisy. Seam lines can trap dirt.
	Rubber is a natural, recyclable material made in tiles and sheets.	Durable, slip resistant. Good sound absorbency. Won't fade.
	Inlaid vinyl The pattern and color run through the whole thickness.	The most durable type of vinyl.
	Standard vinyl Comes in sheet or tile form in a huge range of colors and patterns printed onto the top layer, which will eventually wear out.	Can be slippery when wet and can fade and discolor.

Resilient flooring has long been a popular kitchen choice because it is inexpensive and durable.

ACTION POINTS: using resilient flooring

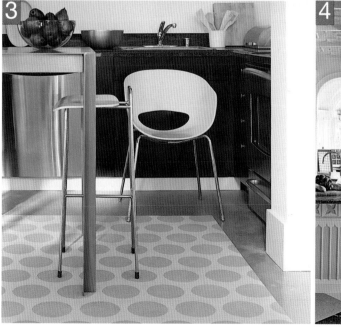

1 GO FOR FOR AN EASY-CARE OPTION. CHECKERED VINYL IS THE IDEAL FLOORING CHOICE FOR THIS HARD-WORKING PANTRY.

2 CHOOSE CHECKS FOR A CLASSIC LOOK. MORE GEOMETRIC BLACK AND WHITE CHECKERBOARD FLOORING, HERE MATCHING THE COLORS OF APPLIANCES AND COUNTERTOPS.

3 STRUCTURE SPACE WITH FLOORING. IN THIS SMALL LOFT APARTMENT KITCHEN, A GRAY AND WHITE VINYL MAT DEFINES THE SEATING AREA—SO SIMPLE AND SO EFFECTIVE.

4 PLAN A PLAID IN TILES. BLACK, GRAY, AND WHITE LINOLEUM CHECKS COMPLEMENT THE REST OF THE DÉCOR IN THIS STRIKINGLY DECORATED KITCHEN.

lights

Good lighting adds a new dimension to a kitchen, making it sparkle in its many different moods. This requires careful planning, as changing lighting arrangements after the room has been set up will be messy and expensive. There are two important strategies: make the most of the natural light, and then give yourself as many options as possible in how you use artificial light.

OPPOSITE: HANG PENDANTS ON LONG CABLES FROM HIGH CEILINGS SO THAT YOU CAN LIGHT AREAS INTIMATELY. ALSO CONSIDER ADDING A LOWERING AND RAISING MECHANISM TO LIGHTS POSITIONED OVER EATING AREAS.

ABOVE: LIGHTS CONCEALED IN THE RECESS REFLECT BRILLIANTLY FROM THE STAINLESS STEEL STOVE FOR A UNIQUE EFFECT.

Sunshine lifts our spirits, and rooms that brim with natural light are inviting and a pleasure to be in. If your kitchen already has large windows, plan around this key feature. There are a number of options to explore if your kitchen doesn't get much of the sun, or is orientated so that it only gets a solar boost at one time of day. The most dramatic is to put in new windows, possibly high up above cabinet level. Although this is a major change, it could transform the room. If there is a mudroom or pantry next to the kitchen, an internal window can be a vehicle for natural light, too. It may be possible to install skylights—a great way to get natural light flooding into the room. If this is impractical, one idea new to the market is a tubular skylight, which is a reflective tube that bounces light down through the roof space and releases it through a fitting in the ceiling. To make the most of the natural light coming in, use plenty of reflective materials (such as stainless steel and chrome), and paint the walls in light colors.

Lighting has three functions (task, ambient, and accent) that can, of course, overlap (see page 102). Kitchens need different lighting at different times of the day. At breakfast time we feel most comfortable in a bright, well-lit room—so you need good general light from the ceiling. An evening meal will be prepared under strong light at the countertop and stove (so you need spotlights under the cabinets), but it will be eaten in a more intimate and softer ambience at the dinner table, calling for the soft glow of a wall sconce, uplight, or a hanging pendant.

It takes careful planning to achieve a good balance of task, ambient, and accent lighting without turning your kitchen into a lighting showroom. Avoid choosing lights just because they are attractive: while a stylish fixture can be a decorative feature, it must meet a genuine lighting need.

It can be fun to plan the lighting so that some, or all, or most sources are hidden, concealed by cabinets, recesses, and valances. Many a kitchen has benefited from the shift away from spotlights toward recessed cans, which one barely notices. You can also playwith lighting to create effects. For example, underlighting from the cabinet base gives an impression of space, creating a "floating" effect.

Ceiling lights

If there is a central ceiling rose in your kitchen, you could use it to house a pendant light to provide some good general lighting. If you need more powerful light in specific directions, consider fitting a ceiling track with spots. A long track allows you to fit several spotlights from which light can be accurately directed or, using a wide beam, provide a more general wash of light—especially if the beam is bounced off a wall to diffuse the light more.

ABOVE: THESE WHITE GLASS SHADES HAVE BEEN HUNG ON OLD-FASHIONED CLOTH CORD IN A MODERN DESIGN THAT HARKS BACK TO THE THIRTIES.

OPPOSITE: LARGE HANGING LIGHT FITTINGS MAKE A MAJOR DESIGN STATEMENT, BUT POSITIONING IS CRUCIAL. HERE, THE SYMMETRICAL ROOM LAYOUT AND CENTRAL ISLAND GIVES THE CHANDELIER A NATURAL HOME.

Lighting terms

choice	what	where
	Task e.g. recessed halogen lights, spotlights. This is the light you need so you can really see what you are doing when cutting and preparing food, cooking it, and washing up.	General around the perimeter of the room, over sinks and cooktops (often hidden in the hood). Over countertops, usually from under the cabinets.
	Ambient e.g. pendants, rise and fall lamps, recessed cans, uplights. Used as general light and to delineate the areas of the kitchen.	Centrally to light the room, and over key areas such as the dining table and the island. Lights behind glass-door cabinets. Possibly also on walls.
	Accent e.g. Recessed cans or spotlights, uplights. Decorative light on shelves and walls designed to pick out things of visual interest. Create intimate pools of light.	Lighting pictures and other features such as collections in cabinets or on shelves.

More difficult to install, but less intrusive, are recessed cans (also available with regular or wide-angle beams), which fit snugly and unobtrusively into the ceiling. If you are fitting new light points and the room is a large one, fitting two pendant lights in different parts of the ceiling might help you define the different areas and roles of the room. A rise and fall pendant over a dining area allows you to switch from a general ambient wash to an intimate pool of light when you are enjoying evening meals.

Wall lights

Wall lighting allows you to change the atmosphere in the room, and can be a way of providing the task lighting so crucial to a kitchen. Direct light up to create a soft effect that emphasizes the height of the room, or down to illuminate an eating zone.

The underside of wall-mounted cabinets is the perfect place to site spotlights to provide task lighting for cooking. If the cabinet doors are made of clear or frosted glass, you could consider lighting the interiors as well, to highlight pretty plates and bowls, or to contribute to the general ambience.

Dimmer time

Of all the rooms in the house, the kitchen needs the most lighting options and these are made far wider when all the light sources can be adjusted with a dimmer switch rather than just being turned on and off. For example, the bright task lights set under cabinets can be transformed into candle-like pools when the meal is served. Do try out dimmer switches as they tend to buzz, which can be intrusive, and double-check that the lamp type selected works with a dimmer (not all do).

Finally, in addition to deciding where the lights should go, consider the location of the switches and if you are going to put any lights onto the same circuit so that they come on and off together. A row of switches can be unattractive and will interrupt the flow of your wall décor: consider placement carefully. You'll want to be able to switch on the ambient lights as you enter the room, so bear this in mind if you usually come in through a back door or via a mudroom.

ABOVE: STAINLESS STEEL
REFLECTS LIGHT SO WELL THAT
YOU CAN AFFORD TO CONCEAL
LIGHT SOURCES AND STILL GET
PLENTY OF LIGHT WHERE YOU
MOST NEED IT.

OPPOSITE: THREE LARGE HANGING
LIGHTS ILLUMINATE THE LIMESTONE
COUNTER, KEEPING THE AREA
INTIMATE DESPITE THE HIGH
CEILING.

ACTION POINTS: lighting

1 MIX LIGHTING SOURCES TO GOOD EFFECT. THE LARGER SPOTS ARE USED TO LIGHT SPECIFIC WORK AREAS WHILE THE SMALLER, TWINKLING BULBS ADD ATMOSPHERE. THE RECESSES ABOVE THE TABLE ARE INDIVIDUALLY LIT TO FORM ATTRACTIVE DISPLAY AREAS.

2 MAKE A STATEMENT. THIS ENAMELED-STEEL HANGING LIGHT IS A MAJOR DECORATIVE FEATURE, ITS CURVES MATCHING THOSE OF THE CIRCULAR MARBLE TABLE BELOW.

3 COMBINE OLD AND NEW. AN ANTIQUE SWEDISH CHANDELIER LIGHTS THE WHOLE ROOM, WHILE THE LAMPS OVER THE STOVE ARE CAREFULLY CONCEALED.

4 TAKE RISKS. SPOTLIGHTS ARE USED TO PROVIDE AMBIENT AND TASK LIGHTING. THEY CAN CLUTTER A FLAT CEILING, BUT HERE THEY SHARE SPACE WITH SLOPING BEAMS TO HAPPY EFFECT.

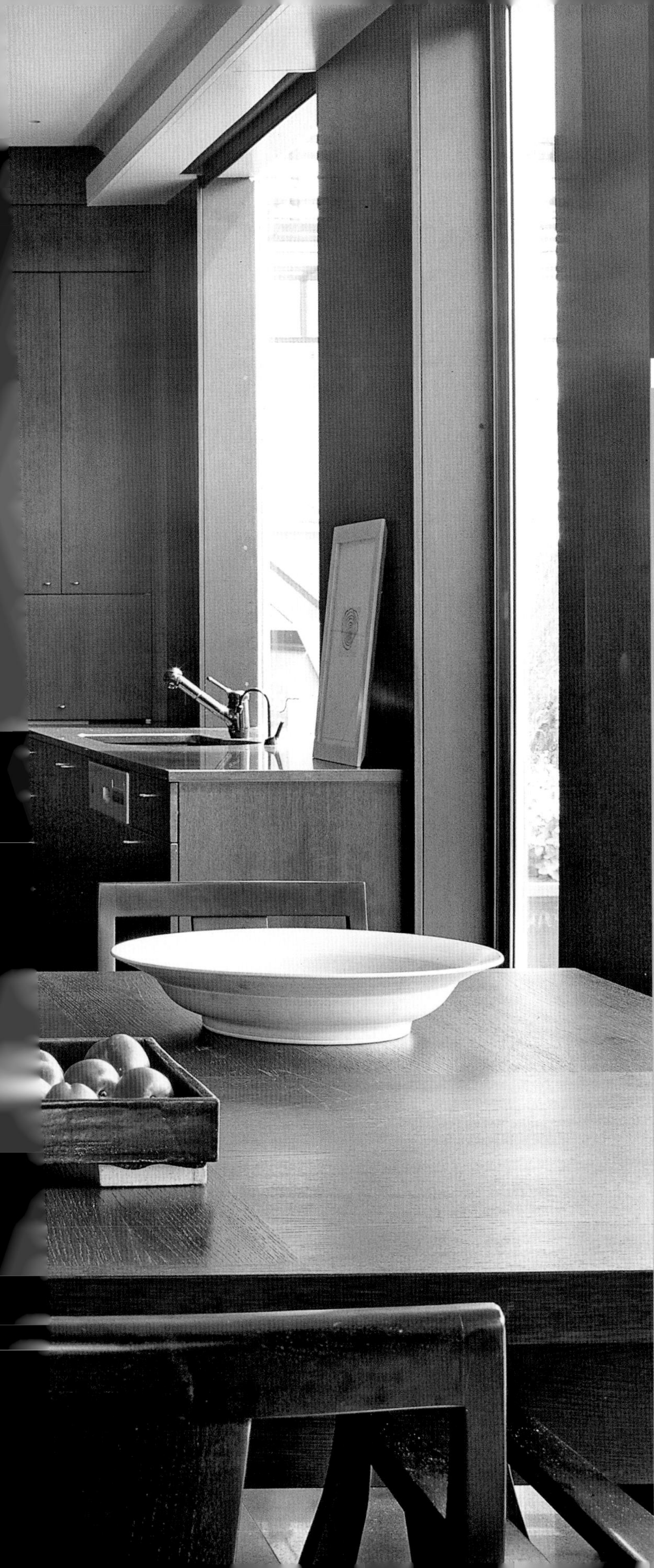

PART 2
decorate

decorative style

ABOVE: BLUE IS CALM AND
EFFICIENT. CHOOSING VARIOUS
SHADES OF THE SAME COLOR IS
A ROUTE TO A SIMPLE, EFFECTIVE
COLOR SCHEME.

OPPOSITE: THINK ABOUT SHAPES
AS WELL AS COLORS. HERE THE
SQUARES IN THE WINDOWS,
CABINET DOORS, AND TILING ARE
BALANCED BY THE ARCHING OF
THE CABINET DOORS AND EXHAUST
HOOD TOGETHER WITH THE
SOFTER CURVES OF THE CHAIRS.

Much of the business of planning a kitchen is concerned with the function of the room. However, an enormous element in the pleasure and success of the end result is in how it looks. It can be difficult to plan the decorative element of a kitchen because sometimes it is hard to picture the room as a whole.

In this part of the book we begin by considering color, the most important influence on the changing moods of the room. We then look at what options are available on the wall (tiles, paint, or paper? Plain or decorative?), and go on to explore the opportunities for window treatments. After that you will find guidance on choosing accessories such as the table and chairs, and whether you want to display items in the kitchen where, after all, you, your family, and your guests spend so much time.

Even more so than with choosing a type of kitchen, decorative style is about you and your family as individuals, and making the room match your personalities. The lovely thing about this is that it is relatively easy to make changes and alter the room as your own personality develops over time. You can even revamp your kitchen every few years for very little expense just by changing some of the colors and accessories.

Because revitalizing the décor is relatively easy, while renovating a kitchen isn't, it is vital that you start with a "canvas" that you are happy with in the form of an attractive, functional kitchen design made with quality components. Get this right and it will last 10 to 20 years. You are likely to change the look of the rest of the room several times during this period as you and your needs change.

color confidence

Color sets the mood. Whatever the style of kitchen you have chosen, the color on the walls will have a major impact on how it looks and feels. Indeed, if you are happy with the layout of your kitchen and feel it just needs freshening up, a quick paint job, and maybe a new set of cabinet doors will be enough to convince many that it is a major renovation, because the whole atmosphere will have changed.

Before going any further, though, some understanding of what color is and how to use it helps inform any decisions you need to make. Interior designers often use the color wheel to identify which colors work well together (see overleaf). The color wheel shows the relationship between the many hues that make up the spectrum.

All colors are mixed from the primary colors: red, yellow, and blue. Equal amounts of these mixed in various combinations produce the secondary colors, such as orange, green, and violet. The infinite number of subtle variations between these hues are the tertiary colors, which allow for so much variation in the range of colors we see. Add white (to lighten into tints) or black (to darken into shades), and you have the complete palette. Since the range of options is infinite, it is a great help to know a few simple "rules" about how to choose colors—even if you end up breaking them.

ABOVE: LINK ROOMS AND ZONES BY USING THE SAME COLORS, AS IN THE YELLOW AND WHITE DINING AREA AND KITCHEN.

OPPOSITE: BOLD COLORS MAKE BIG STATEMENTS. THE ROYAL BLUE PANELS IN THIS KITCHEN STRONGLY DEFINE THE AREA AND ARE DESIGNED TO DRAW VISITORS' EYES AS THEY ENTER THE ROOM.

COMBINE HOT COLORS WITH A
FEW NEUTRAL SHADES TO
PREVENT THE OVERALL
APPEARANCE FROM BECOMING
TOO OVERWHELMING.

• **Neighboring colors on the wheel** are known as harmonizing colors and pair up to create a pleasing, balanced effect—like yellow and pale green. They can be used in different proportions without dramatically affecting the overall result.

• **Opposite colors** contrast with each other for a more striking effect (think of yellow and purple). These are rarely used equally: one color is used for most surfaces but the other is used in small quantities to add interest. In the kitchen, an accent color might be used as a border painted onto cabinet doors, or it may be a piece of equipment, like an orange toaster in a blue room or a pink tea kettle in a green setting.

• **Black and white** do not appear on the color wheel but their addition to any color creates shades (using black) or tints (using white).

• **Adding black to a color** makes it look both darker and more intimate and creates a "shade."

• **Adding white to a color** creates a more airy, lighter effect and is called a "tint."

Colors are also divided into "warm" and "cool" groups, according to how much hot red or cool blue they contain.

For decorating purposes, the group of colors known as neutrals are used extensively because they work with a wide range of colors, having no strong "personality" of their own. Neutrals are whites, off-whites, and subtle shades of yellow and brown. There is also a group of colors known as "naturals" because they echo the hues of nature, such as earth browns or pebble grays.

Most color schemes comprise a main color, which will predominate, with a harmonizing color (which may be used on up to a third of the surfaces) and an accent color (ten per cent or less) for variety. Identifying the main decorative color will allow you to choose harmonizing and accent colors.

Deciding on a color scheme

The most important consideration is how much natural light enters the room. A bright sunny kitchen doesn't need bright sunny colors: the room will feel over-bright and uncomfortable. Lack of light, such as in a north-facing room, will be countered by those bright, sunny colors. Another consideration is the size of the room: a small kitchen will feel even more constricted if the walls are dark, whereas a large area will feel cozier in the same colors.

One nice thing about kitchen color schemes is there are many fewer rules than for other rooms in the house. We tend to prefer our bedrooms to feel relaxed and our living rooms to be elegant, but the kitchen has so many different moods through the day that you can get away with almost anything. Quirky eccentric décor makes for a fun, jolly room, while calm, neutral shades give it restaurant-style chic.

The other great thing about paint palettes is that when, like all décor, they fall out of fashion or just wear out, repainting is a relatively easy and cheap option that most of us can cope with on our own.

Sometimes the most unlikely color combinations work well in a given space if they are of the same tonal value. Toned colors balance with each other. You can judge the tonal value by imagining the colors in a black and white photograph: if they become the same shade of gray, their tone matches. The most important time of day to consider is probably the morning: at breakfast time you will see the décor in natural light. From early to late evening, depending on the time of year, your choice of artificial lighting will highlight or subdue your color scheme.

COMBINING EXOTIC GREEN ON THE WALLS AND FLOOR WITH CALMING WHITE FURNITURE AND ACCESSORIZING IN VERDANT SHADES CREATES A STRONG SENSE OF PLACE.

HIGHLIGHT FEATURES TO CREATE
DEPTH AND INTEREST. PAINTING
THE CABINETS AND WALL ABOVE
THE ARCHWAY IN CREAM
SUCCESSFULLY DRAWS THE EYE
TO THESE PARTICULAR FEATURES.

Paths to the palette

With such a wide range of options, it pays to build up a file of what you like, and sometimes it can be extremely useful to identify what you don't like. Collect pictures from magazines, noting which elements of the design appeal to you. Gather manufacturers' swatches.

There are a number of routes to deciding on the color scheme: taking into account the kitchen style, the rest of the house, the demands of the room, and a favorite color. Certain kitchen styles are traditionally identified with specific colors. Use the table below as a guide.

Even if your kitchen is to include elements of more than one style, think about how much equipment will show. The busier the countertops or shelves, the calmer the backdrop needs to be—there should be some sense of order beyond the clutter. The same applies to ornate finishes: the more curls and flourishes there are, the plainer the color can be to maintain a balance and prevent the effect from being overpowering. If everything but the coffeemaker will be hidden away behind cabinet doors, a deep warm color will prevent the look from becoming so cool as to be unwelcoming. If you keep the fruit bowl well stocked, it will always be a source of bright colors and interesting tones, rather like a vase of flowers in a living room.

Kitchen-style typical palettes

Shaker	• Blues and creams • Gingham checks • Plain white
Country	• Greens, reds and gold
Traditional	• Forest green, brown, mustard yellow
Retro	• Black, red, brown, pink • Exotic accents in turquoise, lime, lavender, or yellow
Contemporary	• Cool, subdued neutrals • Accents in bright, fresh shades

1 THE STRIKING PURPLE ISLAND LIFTS THIS OTHERWISE PREDOMINANTLY CREAM-COLORED KITCHEN.

2 IF YOU OPT FOR A STRONG MAIN COLOR, COMPLEMENT IT WITH WHITE SO THAT IT DOESN'T BECOME OVERBEARING.

3 ZESTY COLORS BRIGHTEN UP THE KITCHEN AND ARE AN ESPECIALLY GOOD CHOICE IN DARK ROOMS.

4 DRAW THE EYE BY REPEATING COLORS, AS WITH THESE BLUE SHADES AND THE CAFÉ STOOL SEAT COVERS.

The starting point

It is useful to have something that helps trigger a color scheme—or two.

Favorite color You could use this as the basis of the color scheme in the room where you spend most of your time. If this is a strong color, such as deep red, experiment with different shades or tints of it.

A favorite feature This could be anything on permanent display, from a bottle-green range that dominates through its sheer size to a bright yellow toaster that cries out for attention. You might gently echo the hue of the range with shades of green, harmonizing turquoise, and a little bit of red accent color. In the case of the yellow toaster, use it as an accent color and go for soft shades of mauve as your main color in the rest of the room, complemented by a subtly tinted white.

Monochromatic scheme Working with shades and tints of one color can be very effective. Remember that kitchens have busy walls and the largest unadorned area will be the ceiling: everywhere else, the color will be broken up by kitchen cabinets or appliances.

Combine finish with color For example, stainless steel is stylish, but cold and unfeeling, so it pairs up well with the balancing warmth of wood or hot colors. While it is tempting to opt for cool, calm shades, they can seem bland without some contrasting brightness. So a calm, restful cream and blue kitchen gets a real boost with a kick of some orange to draw the eye and provide some visual interest—even if the more vivid color is only present in tiny proportions.

A NEUTRAL SETTING OF WHITE, GRAY, AND BLACK ALLOWS THE USE OF VIBRANT ACCENT COLORS SUCH AS THE YELLOW AND MAUVE CABINET DOORS IN THIS CONTEMPORARY KITCHEN.

ABOVE: CONTRASTING BLOCKS OF
BOLD COLORS USED ALONGSIDE
EACH OTHER IS AN UNUSUAL
DESIGN FEATURE. THEY
SUCCESSFULLY GIVE THIS KITCHEN
A REAL SENSE OF IDENTITY.

OPPOSITE: AQUAMARINE
SHELVING FOR WHITE AND GREEN
ACCESSORIES BRINGS THE COLORS
OF THE OCEAN INTO
THIS KITCHEN.

House style

The décor of the house should flow from room to room so that the transition between parts of the house is not jarring. That doesn't mean that they should be the same, but that there should be some elements that are echoed in some way. For example, the rooms may share a wooden floor, or a motif or accent color may appear in both rooms. The rich blue of a dining room, say, will blend well with a paler blue in the adjacent kitchen.

Room style

The shape and dimensions of the room itself are also likely to influence your scheme. If you want to delineate a dining area as separate from where food is prepared, choose a pair of harmonizing colors, one for each section.

Color can also help narrow rooms look more square, large areas more intimate, and enlarge the appearance of small rooms. Darker tones give the impression that the surface is closer to us, so a high ceiling or a distant wall can be made to seem cozier. Lighter tones reflect more light, creating distance, so are good for low ceilings and small rooms.

Possibly the largest influence on your choice of color comes from your existing or proposed new flooring. Checkerboard tile patterns stimulate the eye so need to be balanced by blocks of plain color. A wooden floor brings warmth and textural interest, so you can afford to opt for calm neutrals that won't compete for attention. A flatter finish will encourage the eye to seek interest elsewhere through strong colors or bright accents—and is good for disguising features that you want to hide.

Present company

Another factor will be the colors and textures of the cabinets and appliances that are or will be in your kitchen. For example, a striking, diner-style refrigerator in bright yellow needs either a neutral background so that it is the star of the stage, or an equally strident color, like a bright red, to provide balance. Traditional white was for years the only finish kitchen appliances came in. Now there are many different finishes from bright blue fridges to industrial-style stainless steel ranges to choose from. However, white brings brightness and freshness and is an excellent accent color in any scheme, whether on an appliance or applied to the walls or cabinets.

The color of the cabinets will clearly influence your decisions, too, because they occupy such a large proportion of the room and have a dominant impact on the tone. The stylish warmth of wood creates a subdued, natural look that brings a feeling of

calm practicality and acts as a sympathetic backdrop to almost any style of décor in the rest of the room, from cool shades of white for a minimalist's haven to the zest of a yellow and orange "lift your mood in the morning" design. Given careful preparation, cabinets can be painted to match or contrast with other design elements, and this option allows you to vary their look, too: they needn't be identical. Laminated finishes tend to be bright and glossy, and this often needs to be balanced by tranquil neutrals elsewhere.

Testing out the color scheme

Paint is a great material for trying out ideas (see pages 124–129). Once you have a few thoughts on what might work in your kitchen (don't restrict yourself to one color scheme yet: keep your range of options open), get some test jars of your colors and paint them onto a large piece of paper or board. Try different combinations and experiment with proportions—remember that an accent color might occupy less than 10 percent of the surface and yet still have a major impact. If possible, brush the different colors straight onto the walls (even better, on several walls because they will vary depending on how much light is reflected), and in that way you'll see how they behave in different light and at different times of day.

• **Strong light "flattens" the impact of colors,** so if you have plenty of natural light streaming into the kitchen, you can afford to go for more dramatic shades.
• **Paint colors can dry** to slightly darker or paler shades than when first applied. So always test out your color ideas before painting the whole kitchen.
• **A dark room or corner can look gloomy** and uninviting when painted in a heavy shade.
• **Light bounces off paler colors** so they are great for making small rooms or areas appear bigger as they reflect the light around the room.
• **Don't be afraid to experiment:** some fantastic color schemes break all the rules but look brilliant in their own setting.

ABOVE: PAINT CABINET INTERIORS
A STRONGLY CONTRASTING COLOR
TO ADD DEPTH AND AN ACCENT
COLOR TO AN OTHERWISE
NEUTRAL COLOR SCHEME.

LEFT: GREEN GLASS CABINET
DOORS ADD EXOTIC SPICE TO THIS
STYLISH WHITE AND GRAY KITCHEN
ENVIRONMENT.

walls

Although most of the walls in your kitchen will be concealed behind cabinets and shelves, you still need to decide how to decorate what does show. Walls form the backdrop to whatever is in front of them and in many ways set the tone for the room. A "busy" wall with lots of decorative detail that attracts the eye is perfect if the cabinets and appliances are unadorned. A quiet, neutral wall provides a setting for more ornate, attention-grabbing cabinets and hardware. The choices are paint, paper, tiles, or paneling.

Kitchens are hardworking areas where surfaces get dirty and have to deal with moisture. To help keep your kitchen looking good for the years ahead, choose from specialty paints, which are designed to be more resistant to damp and fungal growth and easy to wash (see overleaf).

Oil-based paints were once the professional's choice because of the high-quality, hardwearing finish they produce. However, there have been massive improvements in the range and quality of latex paint in the last decade. In addition, oil-based paints require mineral spirits or solvent paint thinner for the cleanup, and as they dry, such paints release toxic voltaic organic compounds (VOCs), which are considered to be air pollutants so are best avoided.

Latex paints only need soap and water for the cleanup and they don't smell as strong, so they are more environmentally friendly. Go for good quality paint: it costs a bit more, but gives a better finish that will last longer so you won't have to redecorate as often. Kitchens attract moisture, grease, and other stains: choose durable, washable finishes that will complement your design (see page 126).

THE BURNT-ORANGE WALLS SEEN THROUGH THE DOORWAY DRAW THE EYE ALONG THIS NARROW GALLEY KITCHEN, MAKING THE SPACE SEEM LARGER.

Latex paint finishes

Latex paint is easy to use and it is kind to the environment. A number of finishes are available and they do make a difference to the overall result. For example, shiny finishes (high-gloss and semi-gloss) reflect more light. Try them out first—you may even decide to use a variety of finishes for a subtle textured effect.

High-gloss finish is durable, stain resistant, and easy to clean. It is commonly used on ceilings (for its reflective quality), woodwork, trim, cabinets, and backsplashes. However, it will also show up any flaws in the wall surface and will fade over time.

Semi-gloss is also durable and easy to clean, but it won't lose its sheen and has similar applicatiions to high-gloss.

Satin and eggshell finishes are frequently used on walls and woodwork in high-traffic areas because any flaws can be touched up more easily than with a gloss paint. Although this is a durable finish, it is not resistant to moisture so shouldn't be used close to cooking and washing areas. The finish for both is soft and not shiny.

Flat is a matte finish, very good for concealing flaws such as uneven walls, so it is often used in older properties. This paint is not as easily washable as other finishes.

Decorative painting technique options

choice	what	where
	Checks Created by painting horizontal and vertical stripes (see below), one over the other.	Adds depth and interest to walls. Best in small areas as it can be overwhelming.
	Sponging on Apply a contrasting color over a plain base using a natural sponge.	Creates a soft, dappled look on any large expanse of wall, creating a backdrop.
	Stenciling Dabbed on through a template using a stippling brush that creates a soft textural effect.	Adds a repeating motif— good for borders and cabinet doors.
	Stripes Painted with a roller or, if you have a very steady hand, with a narrow paintbrush. The stripes can be vertical or horizontal.	Makes walls seem taller and adds subtle interest when two very similar shades are used.

Wood-painting tips

If you are painting wood, it needs careful preparation. Any existing coating must be sanded, the wood cleaned, and knots sealed (they leach resin otherwise). Bare wood needs a coat of primer to prepare the surface for painting. Undercoat serves a similar purpose for high-gloss painting. You are then in a position to apply the finishing coat in the color of your choice. If you want to emphasize the grain of the wood, go for a varnish or a colored stain that allows the natural patterning to show through.

Decorative techniques

Unless they are monuments to minimalist industrial chic, most kitchens are very busy on the eye and do not require a striking extra decorative element. However, some paint techniques can enhance the look by softening large areas or adding a touch of flair, and are handy for concealing flaws in the surface of old walls. Special effects can also be used on a small scale to add interest at the back of open shelves, or in small sections of wall exposed between freestanding units, for example.

COMBINE WHITE AND BLACK WITH COLORS DRAWN FROM THE VAST PALETTE OF NEUTRALS FOR A COOL, ELEGANT, AND ULTIMATELY CALMING AMBIENCE.

ACTION POINTS: using paint

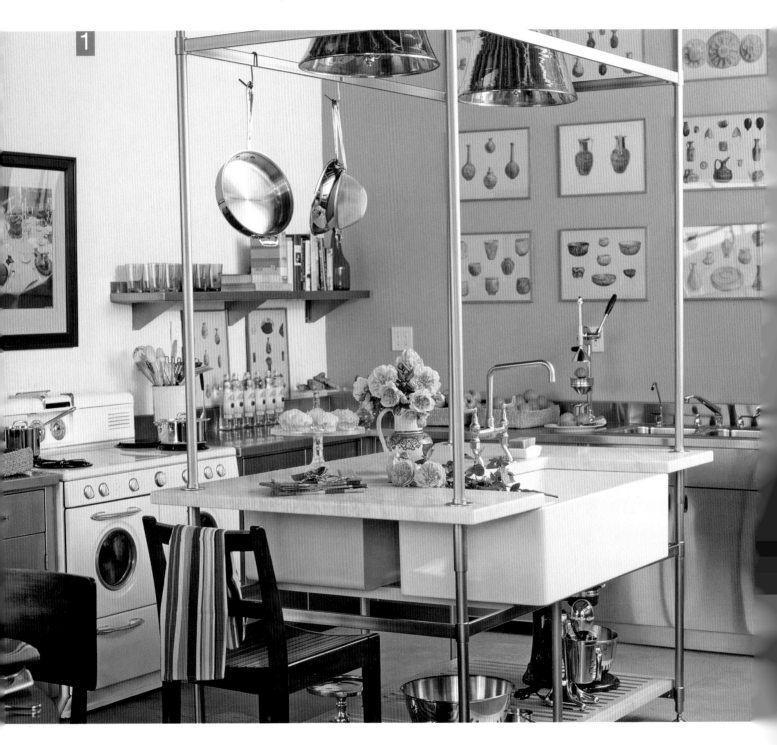

1 CREATE A CLEAN BACKGROUND. THE BRIGHT COLORS OF THE SIMPLE PRINTS ON THE WALL STAND OUT AGAINST A CAREFULLY CHOSEN PALE BLUE BACKDROP. BY PAINTING JUST ONE WALL IN THIS WAY MAKES EVEN MORE OF A FEATURE OF IT.

2 PLAN FOR COLORFUL ACCENTS. BRIGHT RED STOOLS ENLIVEN A PALE GREEN AND WHITE KITCHEN: CONSIDER EXISTING ACCESSORIES WHEN SELECTING PAINT COLORS.

3 USE ANALOGOUS COLORS FOR A HARMONIOUS ROOM. SUNSET COLORS TEAM TOGETHER BEAUTIFULLY HERE WITH THE RED ISLAND BELOW COPPER POTS WHILE THE ORANGE RECESS GLOWS ABOVE THE RANGE.

4 DOWNPLAY DETAILS WITH MATCHING COLOR. DISGUISE POTENTIALLY INTRUSIVE OBJECTS SUCH AS THIS LADDER BY WORKING THEM INTO THE OVERALL WHITE SCHEME SO THAT THEY BLEND IN.

Wallpaper

Hanging wallpaper on a wall that suffers from condensation is not a good idea, but it may be an option in other parts of the kitchen, perhaps on a "focus wall" that is to be left bare or will house some shelving and so requires attractive decoration.

Paper-faced, natural fiber, embossed, and flock wallpapers won't be suitable as they soak up dirt, grease, and odors. However, vinyl and vinyl-coated wallpapers are washable and will resist the mildew that thrives in some damp areas. You don't have to paper the whole wall: large surfaces can be broken up by papering up to chair-rail height, or by using chair-rail molding to create a decorative line. Paper borders are another option for adding a decorative flourish at ceiling or picture-rail height. This allows you to paint the wall different colors on either side of the paper strip, adding depth and interest.

1 DO YOU WANT YOUR KITCHEN TO MAKE A BIG STATEMENT? IF SO, TRY ZEBRA-SKIN WALLPAPER.

2 BEADBOARD LOOKS GREAT WHEN PAINTED BECAUSE THE LINES OF SHADOW ADD TEXTURE TO THE SETTING.

3 PALE BLUE MOSAIC TILES COVER THE WHOLE WALL RATHER THAN BEING USED AS JUST A BACKSPLASH, WHICH WOULD BREAK UP THE ROOM.

Wall tiles

Tiles are easy to clean, waterproof, look hygienic, and come in a vast range of colors and shapes. They needn't be square: other options are hexagons, lozenges, rectangles, and triangles. This is useful because the other kitchen elements tend to create horizontal and vertical lines, and some contrast to this pleases the eye. Even square tiles can be mounted diagonally for a less regimented effect.

One very popular technique is to use mainly plain tiles but with a few patterned inserts, either placed randomly or to create a symmetrical design or border. This can be particularly effective if the inserts stand out in other ways, perhaps by being larger than or a different texture from the other tiles. It only needs a few of these (inevitably more expensive) inserts to transform a bland backdrop into an interesting surface that complements the overall scheme.

Wall tile options

choice	benefits	drawbacks
	Glass tiles Make small spaces appear larger. Available in almost any color, in glossy and etched (matte) finishes.	Glossy finishes smudge easily and need regular cleaning. Adhesive seen through the tile can look blotchy.
	Glazed ceramic Waterproof and durable. Vast range of colors and sizes. By far the most popular choice.	Grouting can discolor or stain.
	Mosaic Choice of stone, ceramic, or glass allows you to choose material that best suits the décor. Finish adds texture to the wall.	Can look too "busy" and must be positioned accurately as flaws show up. Dirt can gather on the large volume of grouting.
	Printed tiles These allow use of motifs and intricate patterns, often combined with plain tiles.	Expensive and can appear a little "lost" from a distance. The motif style may also soon look dated.
	Stone tiles Can be made in marble, limestone, or granite, to complement a stone countertop.	Expensive and can seem over-formal and cold in a kitchen setting.

Kitchen elements tend to create horizontal and vertical lines, so contrasting diagonals and angles please the eye.

Paneling

Wood paneling along a wall or up to chair-rail height is another option. Particularly appropriate to period styles, it provides a sturdy, cleanable, paintable surface that survives the bashes and knocks that come when children are around.

Doors

If you are replacing kitchen doors, consider if you want them to blend or contrast with other wooden surfaces, such as the floor and cabinets. Natural wood feels warm and homey, but painting doors allows you to play with another color element. If the natural light is poor, remove the door altogether, or have it half-glazed in safety glass.

OPPOSITE: YOU GET MORE IMPACT WITH THIS DOOR AS ITS BLACK LACQUER AND ETCHED GLASS HAVE SUCH STRONG PERSONALITY.

BELOW: PANELING'S VERTICAL LINES ACCENTUATE THE HEIGHT OF THE WALL, PAINTED TO MATCH THE OLIVE GREEN CABINETS.

ACTION POINTS: using other finishes

1 EXPLOIT YOUR ASSETS. THE ORIGINAL BRICK WALLS OF THIS EXTENDED HOUSE HAVE BEEN LEFT TO PRESERVE A HOMEY, RUSTIC CHARM.

2 SPLURGE ON A LONG-LASTING FINISH. THESE KITCHEN WALLS ARE COVERED WITH LARGE ANTIQUE LIMESTONE TILES WHOSE PROPORTIONS MATCH THOSE OF THE DARKER-COLORED FLOOR TILES.

3 STAY IN STYLE WITH A CLASSIC LOOK. CEILING BEAMS ECHOING THE BEADED HORIZONTAL BOARDS ON THE WALLS GIVE THIS KITCHEN A RUSTIC FEEL THAT MAKES IT SEEM TIMELESS RATHER THAN CONTEMPORARY.

4 UNIFY WITH MATCHING ELEMENTS. WHITE PANELING ABOVE THE STOVE MATCHES THE CEILING, CREATING A UNIFIED EFFECT THAT ALSO GIVES A GREATER SENSE OF SPACE.

window treatments

See pages 32–33 for guidance on changing windows and their styles. Kitchen windows need careful treatment: they are your eyes on the world during the day and must be allowed to do their main job: letting in light and the view. Sometimes it is tempting to leave the window undressed and let in as much light and scenery as possible. This is great if you don't need privacy after dark, but curtains or shades soften the hard lines of the frames to create a cozier feel in the evening.

Curtains introduce the softness and flow of fabric to the straight lines of a kitchen, adding texture that is often missing. Obviously the style you choose needs to fit in with the rest of the décor and at least one of the colors in patterned curtains should be present elsewhere in the kitchen. Busy patterns will draw the eye and may detract from other features in the room. Fabric in the same or a lighter tone as the walls will make the curtains seem less heavy.

The weight of your chosen fabric will depend on whether they need to offer insulation against drafts—which could be important in the dining area of an older home—but on the whole, kitchen curtains are usually made of fairly lightweight fabric and the formality of interlining isn't usually required.

Kitchen curtains will get dirtier faster than textiles elsewhere in the home, so opt for easily washable fabrics or consider hanging a shade instead. Any fabric hanging near a sink is going to get splashed, so check to see if water stains it. Don't hang curtains near the cooktop or the range for safety reasons.

ABOVE: MAINTAIN CONTINUITY BY HAVING CURTAINS IN THE SAME COLORS AS OTHER DECORATIVE ITEMS, IN THIS CASE THE BLUE AND WHITE CHINA.

OPPOSITE: WHITE LINEN ROMAN SHADES CAN BE RAISED AND LOWERED AS FAR AS IS NEEDED, DEPENDING ON THE TIME OF DAY OR NIGHT.

Finishing touches

Kitchen curtains should complement rather than dominate, so opt for a simple heading style, such as pencil pleats (also known as standard gather), or conceal the heading with a valance or cornice board. A valance—made of fabric—hangs down in front of the curtains, while a cornice—made of wood—is smaller and only frames the heading, creating a less fussy look that better suits most kitchens.

As you'll want to maximize the natural light entering your kitchen, you'll probably want to tie or hold back the fabric during the day, unless you have large windows. This gives a neater finish and is likely to help keep the curtains cleaner for longer. The simplest-looking device is the tieback, which can be made in almost any fabric and is fastened to a hook screwed into the wall. There is also a wide choice of fixed holdbacks.

Hanging systems

Curtain rods Wood or metal, attached to the wall with brackets. Draperies hang from a rod pocket, rings, or tabs, and finials at each end can match the style of other kitchen accessories. Wooden rods suit traditional and country kitchens—and can be painted to blend with the backdrop. Metal rods look more solid.

Tracks Plastic track screwed to the wall. Draperies hang from hooks on gliders. Tracks suit modern-style kitchens, but may need concealing with a cornice or valance elsewhere.

Tension wire Lengths of stretched wire attached to wall fittings. Fabric held in place with clips. Suits very light or sheer fabrics over wide windows. Softens black glass in the evenings, but offers no privacy. Suits contemporary kitchens.

PLEATED FABRIC FRAMES THE
DOORWAY, SOFTENING ITS HARD
LINES, WHILE THE COLORS ECHO
THOSE IN THE FLOOR TILES,
DRAWING THE ROOM TOGETHER.

ABOVE: THE LIGHTER THE FABRIC WEIGHT, THE BETTER FOR PANELS. HERE, THE HEADING HAS BEEN GIVEN MORE INTEREST WITH THE ADDITION OF A NARROW STRIP OF THE WHITE FABRIC WITH BLUE RIBBON APPLIQUÉD ONTO IT.

RIGHT: YOU DON'T ALWAYS NEED TO COVER THE WHOLE WINDOW. HERE LIGHTWEIGHT FABRIC DAMPENS THE SUN'S BLAZE WITHOUT DARKENING THE ROOM.

Panels

Panels are a practical and stylish way of softening light and providing privacy in a kitchen, because they look simple and don't gather dirt and grease. They can be suspended from thin rods or tension wires on tab tops, ties, or clips, or hung at the window as a portière (see opposite bottom). Panels contribute to the look of a kitchen as they form a shield that filters harsh light and eliminates the austere blackness of plain glass at night. Very little fabric is required compared with gathered curtains, so you can afford to spend a little more on a pretty color or complementary texture.

Panel options

choice	what	features
	**Appliqué panel** Translucent sheer decorated with pieces of other fabrics, such as prints or embroidery. Use lightweight fabric in contrasting colors or textures and either stitch on or use no-sew iron-on webbing.	Allows the creation of a unique panel that reflects the kitchen design. The panel needn't cover a window entirely. This one merely covers the bottom half as a means of providing privacy in the daytime.
	**Lace panel** Woven patterned fabric filling the window space. Choose from new or antique lace fabrics and turn under the edges to neaten.	An attractive alternative to nets, the lacy designs allow you to see out of the window, but prevent the outside world from looking in during the day. If white doesn't appeal to you, dye the fabric to an appropriate color.
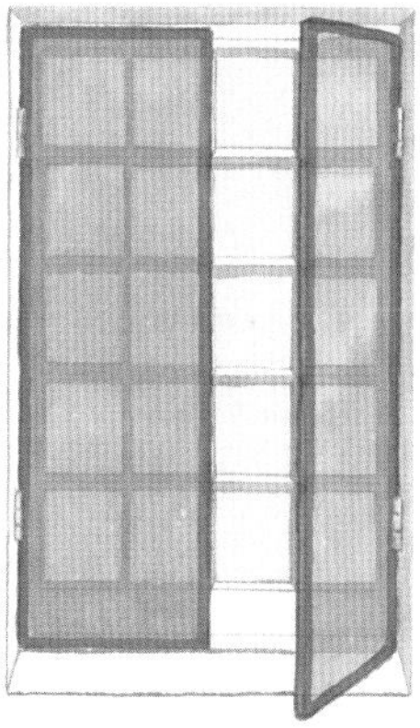	**Portière panel** A thin wooden frame with hinges on the sides and sheer fabric stretched over it. There is nothing to stop you from using either of the ideas in the panels described above on the wooden frames shown here.	Works like a shutter, and so perfect for opening and closing depending on the position of the sun.

Panels are a refreshingly modern finish at any window. Light and airy, they add a hint of color or texture but without being too dominant.

ACTION POINTS: using curtains and panels

1 SOFTEN WINDOWS WITH CURVES. HOLDBACKS TURN EVERYDAY FABRICS INTO ELEGANTLY DRAPED SWATHES THAT BRING THE ROOM TO LIFE.

2 LET IN LIGHT WITH LIGHTWEIGHT FABRIC. THE WHITE DÉCOR SUGGESTS THAT LIGHT CAN BE AT A PREMIUM IN THIS KITCHEN, THEREFORE TRANSLUCENT DRAPES HAVE BEEN USED SO THAT NO NATURAL RAYS ARE BLOCKED.

3 ADD DRAMA TO A DOOR. CURTAINS AND PANELS NEEDN'T BE CONFINED TO WINDOWS—USE THEM ON DOORWAYS, TOO.

4 DRESS UP. THESE HEAVY LINEN CURTAINS LOOK INFORMAL IN THE DAYTIME, BUT ARE SUFFICIENTLY DRESSY TO BE A SUCCESSFUL BACKDROP FOR EVENING DINING.

WITH SPLIT CANE ROLL-UP
SHADES, DAYLIGHT IS FILTERED
THROUGH SO THAT A ROOM
ENJOYS A SENSE OF AIRINESS BUT
WITHOUT THE GLARE.

Cool shades

Many people opt for the clear, clean lines of a shade in the kitchen as these timeless sun shields sit inside the window recess and take up less room than curtains. Shades also have the advantage of being tucked away to the point of invisibility during the day if you wish, although they can be handy for diffusing bright light from a low sun during the day. Shades are less of a fire hazard—an important factor in the kitchen.

Because they fill the large space of the window when drawn down, shades become a major element in the décor, so their materials and design must be considered as part of the overall scheme.
- **Wood, such as bamboo or split cane,** brings a rustic feel.
- **Checked designs of yellow, blue, or red** teamed with white are a classic country look, and can match the tablecloth.
- **Large shades** can take a bold motif.
- **Vertical stripes** elongate the look to make the space seem taller.
- **If your backsplash is a busy pattern,** go for a simpler pattern in similar colors in your fabric choice to complement the backsplash rather than compete with it.
- **To soften the potentially more clinical look of a shade,** use ribbon instead of cord, and add a lace edging.

Shutters

Another option is to have shutters at your windows, which are like miniature doors installed within the window recess that can be swung open and shut. These have an unfussy simplicity that complements any kitchen design, and are available in wood (for a total blackout), sandblasted glass, polypropylene, and metal mesh. They can be a flexible design element because you can shutter just the bottom half of the window for privacy (like café curtains), leaving the space above clear, or shutter the top and bottom separately. Shutters can also be solid or louvered. One drawback of having shutters is that you can't store anything on the window sill because it will block their movement. Furthermore, shutters must be made to measure, so they are not necessarily an inexpensive option.

Shade options

choice	what	features
	**Plain,** such as Roman and roller shades. They lower to form a flat surface so that the fabric can be enjoyed to its full effect. Great care needs to be taken when making from striped or checked fabrics to ensure they are completely vertical and/or horizontal.	The main benefit of a shade such as this is that when they are completely drawn up, they allow in plenty of light. As with all other shades, they can be lowered to whatever height suits you best.
	Ruched, such as Austrian and balloon shades. A fuller shade made in fabric. The folds in the material and gathered frills around three sides create a more opulent effect.	Some fabric is always on display as they don't fold away as much as plain shades. They can be successfully combined with a roller or Roman blind to create a more ornate finish.
	Slatted, such as Venetian or wooden shades. A set of slats that fold flat when drawn up.	Louvers can be angled to allow in some light and are made in a wide variety of colors in addition to simple wood. They suit contemporary kitchens, but gather dust and can be time-consuming to clean.

Many people opt for the clear, clean lines of a shade in the kitchen: it just seems to suit the room better.

ACTION POINTS: using shades

1 TRY A NATURAL SUN FILTER. WHEN THEY ARE PULLED TO THE TOP OF THE WINDOW, SPLIT CANE SHADES ADD SOME TEXTURAL INTEREST TO AN OTHERWISE LARGE EXPANSE OF GLASS.

2 REVERSE DIRECTION. THIS ROLLER SHADE, UNUSUALLY, PULLS UP FROM THE BOTTOM OF THE WINDOW RATHER THAN DOWN FROM THE TOP, WHICH CAN BE USEFUL FOR GIVING PRIVACY WHILE LETTING IN THE LIGHT FROM ABOVE.

3 CHOOSE SENSIBLE SIMPLICITY. A ROMAN SHADE IS AN UNDERSTATED CHOICE THAT WORKS WELL WITH EITHER AN EQUALLY SUBTLE FABRIC, AS HERE, OR MADE FROM SOMETHING MORE DRAMATIC.

4 TIE COLORS TOGETHER WITH TAPES. THIS SLATTED SHADE HAS A PAIR OF FABRIC STRIPS RUNNING ITS FULL LENGTH THAT SOFTEN THE HORIZONTAL LINES AND TIE IT MORE INTO THE KITCHEN'S COLOR SCHEME.

finishing touches

Furnishings and accessories are crucial parts of the look of the kitchen, and are often overlooked at the design stage— but at least they can be changed and adapted throughout the life of the kitchen.

A large dining table can serve as the focus for the room, providing valuable extra preparation space as well as its more obvious function as a place to eat. Wood is the most favored material but the style is important: the homey look of country-style distressed pine might be totally out of place in a retro or minimalist kitchen. Better options could be a marble-topped table to add contemporary chic, or a 1950s laminate affair to complete that retro look.

Dimensions are important: if you already have the table, check that there is space for it in your design, including room for people to move around it and pull out chairs. If you opt for an extendable table to allow for extra diners, look for designs in which the table legs move out as well, otherwise some of your guests will be seated uncomfortably nestling up to a block of wood. If space is a little limited, a circular table can accommodate extra guests more easily than a rectangular one, and round shapes fit into small spaces better than those with straight edges.

Once you've identified where the table will go, consider how it will be lit at different times of day. Also bear in mind how warm its environment is: too near the oven and it will be uncomfortably hot at times, but if it is some way away, especially by a drafty window, it might not be the most welcoming spot and a radiator may be needed.

ABOVE: IT PAYS TO LOOK AROUND FOR IDEAS AND SOURCES. THIS FINE FRENCH FARMHOUSE TABLE HAS BEEN PAIRED WITH SIX FLEA MARKET CHAIRS THAT HAVE BEEN PAINTED AND SKIRTED. NOW THEY SEEM TO HAVE BEEN MADE FOR EACH OTHER!

OPPOSITE: ONE SOLUTION TO A SMALL-SPACE EAT-IN AREA IS TO HAVE A TABLE ON WHEELS. WHEN IT'S NOT NEEDED, JUST STEER IT OUT OF THE WAY. THE BUILT-IN BENCH IS ANOTHER SPACE-SAVER.

Are you sitting comfortably?

If the kitchen is also the venue for entertaining, choose seats for comfort as well as style: sitting on hard chairs with inadequate support for hours is no fun. Padded or woven seats will keep your guests smiling—but the fabric must be able to cope with the odd food or drink spill. Use ties to attach washable seat cushions to chairs.

Barstools look great at a breakfast bar or around a peninsula or island, and are great for informal dining, although you may find it frustrating if they are in line, as people can't face each other, which means that conversation might not flow quite so readily.

Folding and stacking chairs allow for extra guests, but plan for where they will be stored when not needed: a recess in the pantry or mudroom is ideal and keeps them out of the way. Remember that these chairs, like those permanently in the kitchen, should have felt pads added to their feet if they are not to mark a wooden floor. Stop chair feet scraping by fitting rubber tips to the legs.

Benches are a useful option in a small kitchen if the dining area is clearly defined because they can offer extra storage space under a hinged seat. Such a design also lends itself to creating a banquette, which echoes the intimacy of a restaurant booth. This can be a quiet haven with a separate identity from the rest of the kitchen—but climbing in and out can be tricky for less agile guests.

Setting standards

An attractive wooden table needs little adornment—indeed, hanging tablecloth edges don't add a lot of style—but a runner will protect the surface and add some texture and color, if necessary, on top of a simple white or cream cloth. Matching or harmonizing napkins can make the most everyday meal feel a little bit special.

Whether the table is bare or set for dinner, flowers beautify the scene—perhaps your favorite flower or something a little more unusual like little pots of wheat grass or herbs. They look doubly good if displayed in a beautiful vase. Keep the fruit bowl on the table to add color—and encourage healthy snacking.

Evening meals taste much better when eaten by candlelight, but candles are not particularly attractive in the daytime and can become misshapen if exposed to heat, so store them in a nearby drawer.

If you serve a lot of stove-to-table fare, make sure that you have plenty of heat-resistant mats to prevent a disastrous burn, which would be sure to spoil more than one evening at the table!

ABOVE: THE CURVES OF THE STYLISHLY ORNATE CHAIRS ARE A HOMEY ANTIDOTE TO THE MODERN STAINLESS STEEL RANGE.

OPPOSITE: FAUX-BAMBOO STOOLS, A MONKEY VASE, AND CERAMIC BUDDHA ADD A HINT OF EXOTIC SPICES TO THIS SYMMETRICALLY ARRANGED KITCHEN.

Today's kitchens are often used for entertaining as well as cooking, so we want them to reflect our personality.

SMALL DETAILS COUNT. THE DECORATIVE DEVICES IN THIS EATING AREA ARE LEGION, RANGING FROM THE CURLY METAL LEAVES ON THE CHAIR BACKS TO THE UNUSUAL ZIGZAG FINISH AT THE TOP OF THE CABINET AND THE INDIAN METAL LAMPSHADE ABOVE THE CONTRASTINGLY SIMPLE DINING TABLE.

ACTION POINTS: tables and chairs

1 PERSONALIZE MODERN CLASSICS. ALL IS CALM, ALL IS BRIGHT BECAUSE OF THE WIRE REPRO EAMES CHAIRS AROUND THE WOOD AND ALUMINUM TABLE. THE BACK AND SEAT PADS ARE SLOTTED OVER THE METAL FRAMES FOR ADDED COMFORT.

2 MAKE THE MOST OF YOUR SPACE. BUILT-IN BENCHES CREATE EFFICIENT SEATING SPACE AROUND THE WHEELED DINING TABLE, MAKING THE MOST OF THIS COMPACT ROOM END.

3 COZY UP IN A CIRCLE. WHEN SHORT OF SPACE, GO FOR A CIRCULAR TABLE — YOU WILL FIND IT EASIER TO MOVE AROUND THIS SHAPE.

4 PAINT CHAIRS TO MATCH. WOODEN CHAIRS CAN READILY BE CUSTOMIZED TO MATCH EACH OTHER AND ENHANCE THE COLORS USED IN THE REST OF THE KITCHEN.

On display

OPPOSITE: WHILE IT'S NICE TO BE ABLE TO DISPLAY PLATES AND OTHER PIECES OF CHINA ON OPEN SHELVES IN THE KITCHEN, THERE ARE TIMES WHEN IT'S GOOD TO HIDE THEM AWAY WHILE EATING. THAT'S WHERE A PAIR OF CURTAINS SUSPENDED ACROSS THE ROOM, SUCH AS THESE, COME IN USEFUL.

1 GROUP SETS TOGETHER FOR MAXIMUM EFFECT, LIKE THE SET OF PLATES ABOVE THE WINDOW, THE MATCHING CANISTERS IN THE CORNER SHELF UNIT, AND FRESH PRODUCE ON THE MARBLE COUNTERTOP.

2 WHEN HANGING SPACE IS SHORT, HANG PICTURES AND PLATES ABOVE A DOORWAY AS THIS CAN OTHERWISE ALL TOO OFTEN BE A WASTED AREA.

3 OPEN SHELVING IS A CLASSIC FRENCH WAY OF DISPLAYING COLLECTIONS LIKE THESE PLATES AND POTTERY.

Today's kitchens are multipurpose and are often a scene for entertaining as well as cooking, so we want them to be visually stimulating and to reflect our own personality. Consequently, it is worth considering setting aside some space or areas for display. The obvious starting point is the walls, on which can be hung paintings and photographs, plates, and children's artwork (which takes on a new status if mounted in a frame).

If you have a collection of any objects of beauty, from novelty coffee pots to shells gathered on the beach, give them some space. Unless a single item is of outstanding interest, consider grouping things for more visual interest.

You may decide on a food theme, say: pictures of foods; or even layers of multi-colored pasta or beans in a glass jar can be a witty and appropriate decorative addition. You may have some pretty porcelain or colored glassware, or kitchen equipment that is attractive in its own right, such as copper pans or an engraved pitcher. Unused space above cabinets is also ideal for displaying plates or other favorite collections. Prevent them falling by nailing a strip of beading parallel to the wall so that nothing can slip off—raised edges will do the same job on shelving. Just a few touches such as this can bring a kitchen to life, especially if you are able to position objects around the room to draw the eye.

Be aware of how colors sit together. Collections of objects based on a single color theme work especially well, or group them by shape or use, such as vases or jugs. You might want to think, too, about how such items should be lit as this can add an extra dimension—for example, lighting from underneath will make them look dramatic and produce unusual shadows, or positioning a spotlight over them will give them a chance to shine.

PHOTOGRAPHY CREDITS

The publisher would like to thank the following photographers for supplying the pictures in this book:
(**b** = bottom, **c** = center, **l** = left, **r** = right, **t** = top)

Page 1 Jonn Coolidge; **2** John M. Hall; **3** William Waldron; **4** John M. Hall; **6** Jeremy Samuelson; **7** Gordon Beall; **8** Jonn Coolidge; **10** Jean-Francois Jaussard; **11** Keith Scott Morton ; **12** Jonn Coolidge; **13** Jacques Dirand; **14 l** David Montgomery ; **14 r** John Ellis; **16** Michael James O'Brien; **17** Tim Street-Porter; **18 l** Andreas von Einsiedel ; **18 r** William Waldron; **19** Tria Giovan; **20** Fernando Bengoechea; **21** Anthony Cotsifas; **23 tl** William Waldron; **23 tr** Ellen McDermott; **23 bl** Bill Holt; **23 br** Andreas von Einsiedel; **24** Simon Upton; **25** Grey Crawford; **26** Kenny Johnson; **27** Eric Piasecki; **28 t** Lambros Photography Inc; **28 b** Tim Street-Porter; **29** Peter Murdock; **30** Paul Whicheloe; **31** Oberto Gili; **32 t** Tim Beddow; **32 c** Pieter Estersohn; **32 b** Tria Giovan; **33** Jonathan Wallen; **35 l** Victoria Pearson; **35 c** Jeff McNamara ; **35 r** Vicente Wolf; **36** Jonn Coolidge; **38** Karyn R Millet; **41 tl** Antione Bootz; **41 tr** Erik Kvalsvik; **41 bl** Pieter Estersohn; **41 br** Christopher Baker; **42** David Montgomery ; **45** Eric Piasecki; **46** Tria Giovan; **47** Jonn Coolidge; **49 l** Oberto Gili; **49 r** Pieter Estersohn; **50** Lisa Romerein; **51** Ellen McDermott; **52** Tria Giovan; **53 t** Oberto Gili; **53 bl** Erik Kvalsvik; **53 br** John M. Hall; **54** Frances Janisch; **55 t** Michael Grimm; **55 b** Pieter Estersohn; **56** Paul Whicheloe; **57 t** Ellen McDermott; **57 c** Ellen McDermott; **57 b** Victoria Pearson; **58** Eric Piasecki; **59** Lizzie Himmel; **60 l** John M. Hall; **60 r** Dominique Vorillon; **62** Dominique Vorillon; **63** Pieter Estersohn; **64** Jonn Coolidge; **66** Tria Giovan; **67 t** Grey Crawford; **67 bl** Susan Gilmore; **67 br** Karyn R Millet; **68** Tria Giovan; **69** Eric Piasecki; **70** Dominique Vorillon; **71 l** Frances Janisch; **71 r** Simon Upton; **72** Pieter Estersohn; **73 t** William Waldron; **73 bl** Tim Beddow; **73 br** Jonn Coolidge; **74** Jonn Coolidge; **75** Lisa Romerein; **76** Laura Moss; **77** Laura Moss; **78** David Montgomery ; **79** Jonn Coolidge; **80** Eric Boman; **81 t** John M. Hall; **81 bl** Tria Giovan; **81 br** Jonn Coolidge; **82** Tria Giovan; **84** Eric Piasecki; **85 t** Courtesy of Thomasville; www.thomasville.com; **85 bl** Courtesy of Thomasville; www.thomasville.com; **85 br** Eric Piasecki; **86** Jeremy Samuelson; **87** Don **91 bl** Michael Skott; **91 br** Jonn Coolidge; **92 l** Paul Schlismann; **92 r** Timothy Hursley; **93** Jeff McNamara; **94** Simon Upton; **95 t** Roger Davies; **95 bl** Gridley and Graves ; **95 br** Courtesy of Wood-Mode Fine Custom Cabinetry; **96 t** Victoria Pearson; **96 c** Paul Whicheloe; **96 b** Victoria Pearson; **98** Eric Boman; **99 t** Tria Giovan; **99 bl** Dominique Vorillon; **99 br** Dominique Vorillon; **100** Photo: Richard Bryant/Arcaid Architect: Calvin Tsao and Zack McKown; **101** John M. Hall; **102** Ellen McDermott; **103** Eric Piasecki; **104** Jack Thompson; **105** Oberto Gili; **106** Matthew Milman; **107 t** Santi Celeca; **107 bl** Gordon Beall; **107 br** Pieter Estersohn; **108** Peter Margonelli; **110** Christophe Dugied ; **111** Anthony Cotsifas; **112** Ellen McDermott; **113** Peter Murdock; **114** John Ellis; **115** Dana Gallagher; **116** Laura Moss; **117 tl** Andreas Trauttmandorff; **117 tr** Dana Gallagher; **117 bl** Jonn Coolidge; **117 br** Simon Upton; **118** Courtesy of Poggenpohl U.S.; 800-987-0553; www.poggenpohl-usa.com; **121** David Prince ; **122** Simon Upton; **123** Dana Gallagher; **124** Roger Davies; **125** Gordon Beall; **126** Dana Gallagher; **127** Oberto Gili; **128** Victoria Pearson; **129 t** Oberto Gili; **129 bl** Victoria Pearson; **129 br** Fernando Bengoechea; **130 l** Eric Piasecki; **130 c** Peter Murdock; **130 r** Antoine Bootz; **132** Firooz Zahedi; **133** Fernando Bengoechea; **134** Tria Giovan; **135 t** Jonn Coolidge; **135 bl** John Gould Bessler; **135 br** Karyn R Millet; **136** Sheva Fruitman ; **137** Steven Randazzo ; **138** Laura Moss; **139** Victoria Pearson; **140 l** Susan Gentry McWhinney; **140 r** Susan Gentry McWhinney ; **142** William Waldron; **143 t** Eric Piasecki; **143 bl** Tim Street-Porter; **143 br** Ellen McDermott; **144** Oberto Gili; **146** Tim Street-Porter; **147 t** Victoria Pearson; **147 bl** Karyn Millet; **147 br** Jonn Coolidge; **148** Michael James O'Brien; **149** Tara Striano; **150** Grey Crawford; **151** William Waldron; **152** Tim Street-Porter; **154** Pieter Estersohn; **155 t** John Ellis; **155 bl** Eric Roth; **155 br** Nejelko Matura; **156 l** Oberto Gili; **156 c** Jonn Coolidge; **156 r** Susan Gentry McWhinney; **157** Alec Hemer.

INDEX

Page numbers in *italics* refer to illustrations.

Evelegh, ~~Tessa~~.

House beautiful
design & decorate.

$24.95

DATE		
MAR 2 4 2009		
JUL 0 9 2009		
FEB 2 2 2011		
MAR 1 8 2011		
SEP 2 3 2011		
NOV 0 1 2013		
APR 2 6 2018		